HOW TO MAKE REPEAT PATTERNS

A GUIDE FOR DESIGNERS, ARCHITECTS AND ARTISTS

Paul Jackson

LAURENCE KING

Published in 2018 by
Laurence King Publishing Ltd
361–373 City Road
London EC1V 1LR
United Kingdom
T +44 (0)20 7841 6900
F + 44 (0)20 7841 6910
enquiries@laurenceking.com
www.laurenceking.com

This book was produced by
Laurence King Publishing Ltd, London

A catalogue record for this book is available
from the British Library

ISBN: 978-1-78627-129-7

Designed by Nicolas Pauly and Maria Hamer
Printed in China

HOW TO MAKE REPEAT PATTERNS

A GUIDE FOR DESIGNERS, ARCHITECTS AND ARTISTS

Paul Jackson

LAURENCE KING PUBLISHING

Contents

Introduction

Look around you. Look at the floor, the walls and the ceiling, at the furnishings, the decor and the view through the window. Much of what you see will include a two- or three-dimensional motif used a number of times to create a repeat pattern. These repeat patterns are sometimes decorative, like the designs on printed fabrics; sometimes functional, like the positioning of keys on a computer keyboard; and sometimes a combination of the decorative and the functional, like ornamental brickwork.

But how do we create repeat patterns? This book, written especially for designers, will give you the answers. The key is to understand the rules of symmetry. Since there are just four basic symmetry operations – Rotation, Translation, Reflection and Glide Reflection – the rules are easy to learn. These rules can be combined to make more complex symmetry operations, which can be applied with endless creativity to make one type of rotational pattern, seven distinct types of linear patterns (patterns that repeat in a line) and seventeen distinct types of planar patterns (patterns that repeat horizontally and vertically across a flat plane). Each of these patterns is explained here. The book also explains how to tile polygons, how to create complex Escher-like repeats and how to create intricate wallpaper-type patterns that appear to repeat seamlessly.

Symmetry is a rich and complex branch of mathematics. However, most designers would not understand a discussion of symmetry between mathematicians, so this book attempts to strip away the maths and lay bare symmetry as a visual subject, accessible to even the least experienced and maths-phobic reader. It reveals pattern making to be immensely creative, fun and surprisingly simple, with many little-used but wonderful possibilities.

Whatever your level of design experience, whatever materials you wish to use and whatever your special field of interest – from designing textile prints to architectural facades – this book will tell you, in simple language, everything you need to know about creating repeat patterns.

Paul Jackson

What Is a Repeat Pattern and What Is Not?

This is the obvious question to ask at the beginning of a book about how to make repeat patterns. Fortunately, it has a simple answer with one interesting exception, discussed below.

What Is a Pattern?
A pattern is an arrangement of visual elements on a surface.

What Is a Repeat Pattern?
A repeat pattern is created when those elements are repeated according to one of the symmetry operations described in this book.

However, in everyday English the word 'pattern' is sometimes used when 'repeat pattern' would be more accurate. For example, someone will say, 'That scarf has a beautiful pattern,' when they actually mean, 'That scarf has a beautiful repeat pattern.'

Is this is a repeat pattern or not? The spaces between the letters increase incrementally, so there is clearly some repetition of a predetermined operation, but the line of letters itself does not show visual repetition. Any form of scaling (that is, making something larger or smaller) or spacing of visual elements could be described as a repeat pattern or not, depending on how strictly the definition is interpreted. The choice must be yours.

aa a a a a a a a

This is a pattern of letters arranged randomly within a square. It is not a repeat pattern, but a collection of graphic forms.

When a symmetry operation is performed on the same arrangement of letters, the result is a repeat pattern. Here, the arrangement is rotated around a point (rotational symmetry), repeated along a line (linear symmetry) and made into a grid (planar symmetry). The book will explain these three forms of pattern making in detail.

Cell

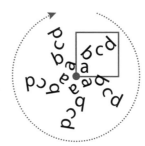

Rotational symmetry

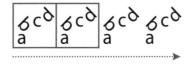

Linear symmetry

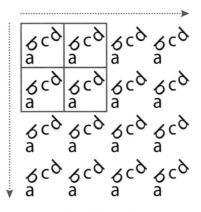

Planar symmetry

Repetition, Elements, Motifs and Meta-motifs

A repeat pattern is composed of up to four parts, discussed here. Not all of them need to be used to create a repeat pattern.

An Element
An element is the 'atom' of a repeat pattern: its smallest indivisible component.

Elements

An element can be simple, complex, abstract, representational, black and white, multicoloured, two-dimensional, three-dimensional, one material, many materials … without end. In this book, elements are usually asymmetrical letterforms (see page 16 for a more detailed explanation of why letterforms were chosen).

Repeat patterns can be made using elements only. To create a repeat pattern, it is not always necessary to create a motif or mega-motif (described on the opposite page), but an element is essential.

The element used in this section of the book is the lower case letterform g. Note that it is asymmetrical, meaning that no line can be drawn through it so that the shapes are the same on each side. The g is shown here at different rotations. Any one of these (or a different one) could become an element.

A Motif

A motif is the 'molecule' of a repeat pattern, composed of two or more elements. The elements can be arranged in a near-infinite number of motifs, depending on the number of elements and whether, for example, they are arranged randomly or in a repeat pattern.

The element, the lower case letterform g, is arranged randomly or in carefully organized repeats to create a few of the many possible motifs. Each one of them could create a near-infinite number of repeat patterns. When many possible motifs are multiplied by a near-infinite number of repeat patterns, we already have more possibilities for patterns than anyone could possibly design in a lifetime.

Element

Sample motifs

A Meta-motif

Two or more motifs can be combined to create a meta-motif, which can then be used to create a repeat pattern. As before, the number of possibilities is immense.

The first of the sample motifs from the previous section is used here to show a few of the ways in which it can be repeated to create meta-motifs. As before, the same motif can be used to create different meta-motifs in an immense number of ways.

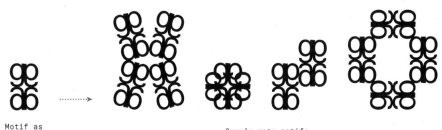

Motif as
element

Sample meta-motifs

Symmetrical Repetition

Once the element, motif or meta-motif has been created, it can be used to generate a repeat pattern, using one or more of the four basic symmetry operations explained in Chapter 1. These symmetry operations form the basis of this book.

Repetition, Elements, Motifs and Meta-motifs

There are three ways in which the elements, motifs, meta-motifs and symmetry operations can combine to create a repeat pattern. Here are those three ways, explained in detail.

One Element + Symmetry Operation
= Repeat Pattern
In this most direct of methods, a single element is repeated to create a repeat pattern. The pattern is made using any of the four symmetrical operations listed on page 21. Note that only one element can be used. If a second is included, the element becomes a motif.

The element here is the lower case letterform g. In this example, the repeat pattern is created by translation (see page 26). However, any of the four symmetry operations could have been used as the example. The repeat pattern could also have been created by tiling the surface (see page 111).

g

Element

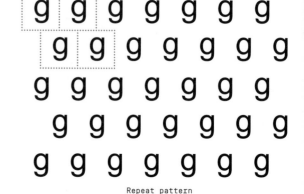

Repeat pattern

Motif + Symmetry Operation
= Repeat Pattern

In this method, a number of elements are combined to create a motif. This motif is then repeated using any of the four symmetry operations to create a repeat pattern.

The g element is reflected horizontally and vertically to create a symmetrical motif of four elements. In this instance, the motif was repeated across the surface by translation to create the repeat pattern, though any of the four symmetry operations could have been used.

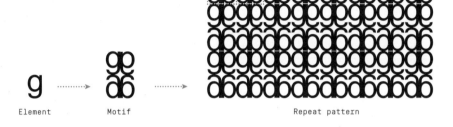

Element   Motif   Repeat pattern

Meta-motif + Symmetry Operation
= Repeat Pattern

It is possible to combine identical motifs as though each one was an element in order to create a meta-motif that can then be repeated using any of the four symmetry operations. This process, of creating ever-larger and more complex meta-motifs from smaller motifs or meta-motifs used as elements, can be taken through many iterations.

The motif from the previous image is used here as an element to create a meta-motif. The meta-motif is then repeated across the surface by means of translation, though any of the four symmetry operations could have been used. Note how even though the same motif is used, the use of the motif as a meta-motif creates a more complex repeat pattern.

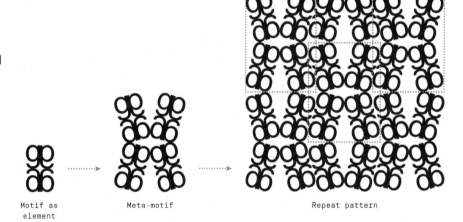

Motif as   Meta-motif   Repeat pattern
element

Cells and Tiles

Cells and tiles are similar-looking – sometimes even identical – and do the same job. They are the polygons that enable areas of pattern to fit together and repeat across a surface. Without them there would be no repeat patterns.

The difference between cells and tiles is that the boundary of a cell is defined by a pre-designed element, motif or meta-motif, whereas the boundary of a tile is defined before an element, motif or meta-motif is designed. Cells contain a graphic image: tiles are blank. They are introduced here, but both cells and tiles are discussed in detail later in the book.

Cells

The red polygons define the edges of a cell. Most cells are simple polygons that fit together without spaces in between them. They define the limits of an element, motif or meta-motif, or define the limits of a sequence of symmetry operations, especially in planar patterns, as described in Chapter 3. A cell can fit tightly around an element, motif or meta-motif to create a dense repeat pattern, or it can leave a space, so that the graphic images have space between them.

The same element, motif or meta-motif can fit into any polygonal cell: for example, the 'd' motif seen on this page is used in cells that are triangular, square, rectangular and hexagonal. The shape of the cell and the size of the graphic image within will determine the repeat characteristics of the pattern. The cells illustrated here are a few of the many possible examples. As you read through Chapter 3, you will discover many more.

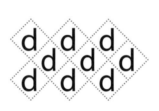

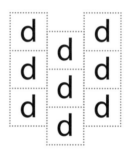

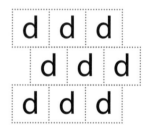

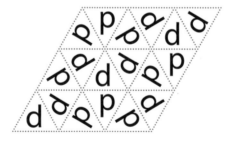

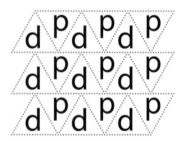

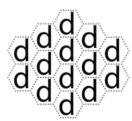

Tiles

Tiles are blank cells. In this book, they are bounded by black lines to differentiate them from red-walled cells. Whereas the shape of a cell can be defined by the element, motif or meta-motif it contains, the creation of a tile can either precede any consideration of the graphic images it will contain, or the repeat pattern can be made solely from the tiles themselves, without any graphic content.

The tiles illustrated here show a selection of the near-infinite number of ways in which tiles can be made, which are explained in detail in Chapter 4. It shows tiles made from a single polygonal shape, or from two shapes, polygons that fit together without spaces and polygons that do not fit together, leaving secondary polygonal spaces between them. Whereas cells are usually simple, tiles can be complex and creatively designed.

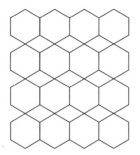
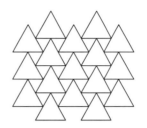
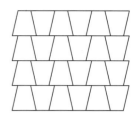
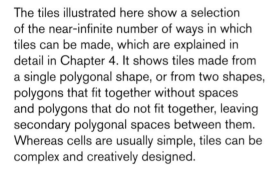
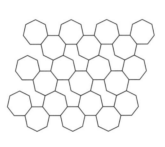
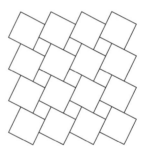
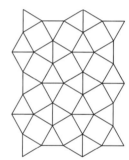

Letterforms as Elements

Each section in the book uses a different element. For visual consistency, the elements are almost always asymmetrical upper case or lower case letters from the Roman alphabet. A symmetrical letterform is used only once (on pages 64–65) when it is particularly relevant to the symmetry operation.

Being asymmetrical, the letters have no line of symmetry. So, for example, letters such as A, B, C, I, v and w are ineligible, because one half of the letter reflects the other half. Letters such as m, n and u are asymmetrical, but only marginally so, and were therefore also excluded from the list. The letters b, d, p and q are reflections of each other, but because they are clear and simple asymmetrical forms and thus ideal for demonstrating the principles of pattern making, they are used in the book.

By using an asymmetrical letterform, it becomes clear when one of the four symmetry operations has been performed on it, because the letter can be seen to have been rotated, translated or reflected. A symmetrical letterform would not always reveal such actions. However, when designing your own element, there is no reason why it should not be symmetrical.

Letterforms are used throughout the book because they are neutral symbols of how patterns can be created. They side step the use of elements that could be described as Japanese, Art Deco, Celtic, Aboriginal and many other distinctive visual styles because such patterns could make the book appear to be a book of pattern sources, which it is not.

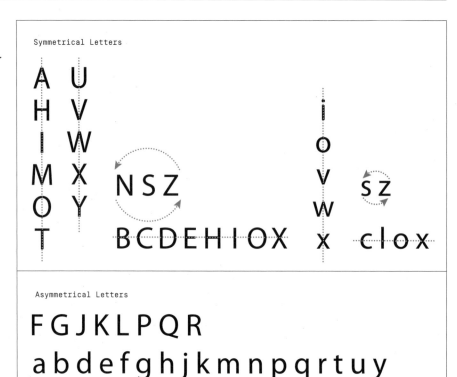

Here, the 26 letters of the alphabet are shown in their upper and lower case forms, grouped into different categories of symmetry: horizontal reflections, rotations, vertical reflections and asymmetrical letterforms.

As stated opposite, asymmetrical letterform elements are used throughout the book because of their graphic neutrality. It is very important to remember, however, that elements, motifs and meta-motifs can be anything of your choosing. For example, they can be simple spots or stripes or complex florals; monochrome or multicoloured; embossed or etched; photographic or hand-drawn; scanned or computer-manipulated; or even potato prints. The only limit is your imagination.

You, dear reader, have a responsibility as a designer of any level of experience and of any specialism to push the boundaries of what may or not be an element or a repeat pattern, to experiment, to be unafraid of trying and failing, to invent and to create great repeat patterns that combine knowledge with innovation. For these reasons, you are encouraged to read the book in detail and with care. Deep learning does not come from skimming through the pages.

Among the things that a computer can do exceptionally well is to copy and paste, to rotate and reflect, and to move an object a specified distance. Any graphic software will have these functions, even basic freeware. These operations work together to make the creation of repeat patterns by computer quick and simple. In no time, a designer can try many variations of colour, pattern and scale, even trying different symmetry operations to see how they look.

Relatively low-tech methods that create repeat images should not be dismissed. Photocopiers can quickly generate great-looking black-and-white or colour images that can be imported into a computer and manipulated to create a repeat pattern with interesting surface textures. The same applies to linocut prints, monoprints, photographs, discarded ephemera, rubbings, found objects and more. The computer is a wonderful tool, but it is not the only tool. Other methods may seem old-fashioned or limited by comparison, but they can yield graphic effects that are difficult to generate digitally.

As with any area of design, there are many advantages to thinking originally, to using unlikely materials and to finding unusual methods of production. Try to think of your computer as the last resort, not the first.

How to Read this Book

The book should be read somewhat like a novel: if it is read in page order from the first page to the last, the full depth of the story and how its leading characters relate will be revealed and understood. To jump to and fro or to dive eagerly into one of the later chapters will inevitably lead to some frustration. A glossary is provided at the back to help explain any technical terms that might have been skipped over.

Some of the symmetry operations – particularly in Chapter 3, which introduces the seventeen planar symmetry operations – are relatively complex, composed of a sequence of specific geometric twists, turns and rotations that an Olympic gymnast would envy. The best way to learn them is to create your own examples with pencil and paper or, if you have access to a computer with CAD software, to use the copy, paste, move, rotate and reflect commands to recreate the sequence of transformations.

Perhaps, then, simply to 'read' the book is not the best way to use it after all. Time spent making examples will significantly increase your understanding of the potential of each of the symmetry operations.

How the Book Is Structured
The book is divided into two parts. The first part, comprising Chapters 1–3, describes the four basic symmetry operations, and shows how these operations can be used and combined to create one rotational symmetry operation, seven linear symmetry operations and seventeen planar symmetry operations. This represents the full set of all possible symmetry operations in zero, one and two dimensions. Just why this is the full set and why there can be no other symmetry operations has a complex mathematical explanation that is beyond the scope of this book to explain. (Although there are no other operations, there are others that may at first glance appear to be different. However, under close mathematical scrutiny they will be shown to offer nothing new.) For easy reference and comparison, the full set of linear and planar symmetry operations is grouped together towards the back of the book on pages 154–157.

The second part of the book, chapters 4 and 5, introduces a wider and somewhat less rigorous view of how to make repeat patterns, beyond the finite set of symmetry operations.

Chapter 4 introduces the concept of the tile and shows how tiles can be used to cover a plane, either fully or with gaps that become secondary tiles.

Chapter 5 introduces the complex tiling techniques of the Dutch graphic artist M.C. Escher, explaining how interlocking tiles of geometric shapes can evolve to resemble animals, birds, human figures and more. Although the results can be remarkably lifelike and seem incomprehensibly clever, the method of making these tiles is surprisingly intuitive and fun, once a few simple principles are understood. Chapter 5 also introduces the technique of making seamless repeats, typically seen on wallpapers, in which the repeat has no apparent edge or border.

Throughout the book, spreads of repeat patterns appear that make creative use of what was introduced in the preceding pages. These spreads are not intended to be a source of patterns to copy, but are included to show the potential of different pattern-making techniques beyond the letterform examples used throughout the book.

Zero, One and Two Dimensions Explained

The book makes extensive reference to zero, one and two dimensions. What do these terms mean and how do they relate?

One point – an infinitesimally small dot – is a singularity. It has no length, depth or width. The point is zero-dimensional. With reference to symmetry, this is rotational symmetry, in which the symmetry operation is repeated around a point. It is explained in Chapter 1.

Two points at a distance apart create a line. The line is one-dimensional. With reference to symmetry, this is linear symmetry, in which the symmetry operation is repeated along a one-dimensional line. It is explained in Chapter 2.

Three points at a distance apart create a triangle on a flat plane. The plane is two-dimensional. With reference to symmetry, this is planar symmetry, in which the symmetry operation is repeated across a two-dimensional plane. It is explained in Chapter 3.

(It is also possible to have four points, by suspending a fourth point somewhere in space above the triangle. When all the points are connected, a solid form with four triangular faces is created, called a tetrahedron. It is three-dimensional. Three-dimensional symmetry operations are significantly different from point, line and planar symmetry operations and are not discussed in this book.)

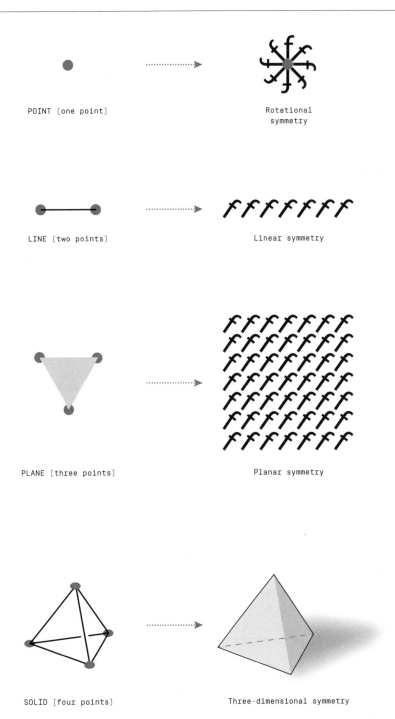

POINT [one point]

Rotational symmetry

LINE [two points]

Linear symmetry

PLANE [three points]

Planar symmetry

SOLID [four points]

Three-dimensional symmetry

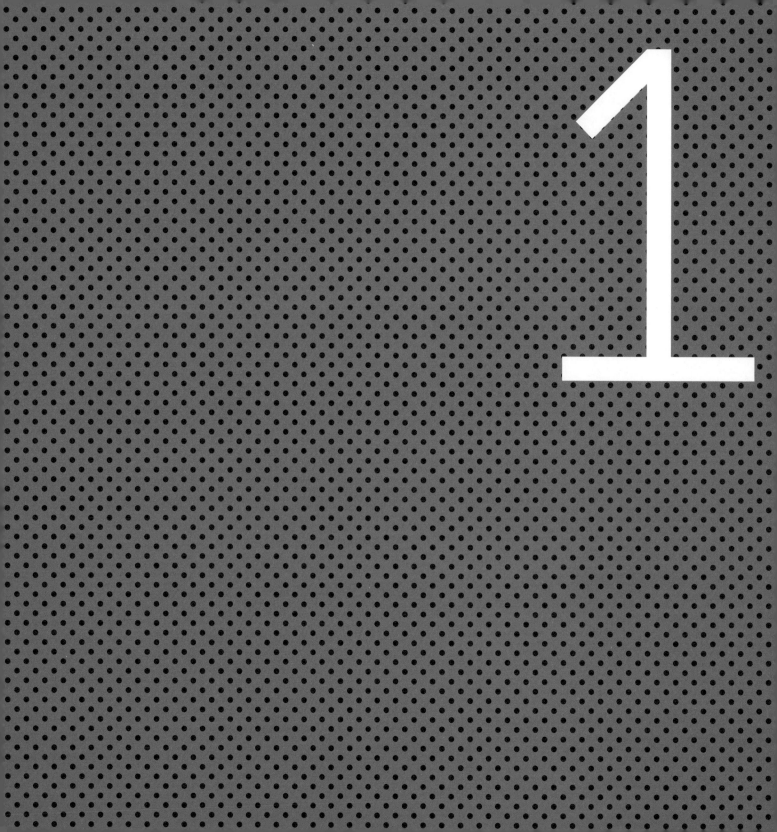

1. The Four Basic Symmetry Operations

'Symmetry' – as it concerns the making of repeat patterns on a surface – can be generally defined as occurring when a shape is copied and the duplicate is slid, rotated or reflected relative to the original.

The world of symmetry is as wide and rich as the human imagination, but it is built on just four basic principles. These principles, the basic language of all symmetry, are easy to learn and offer a wonderfully rich environment of creativity, even without moving on to the later chapters in which they are explored in combination. So, please linger here a good while before moving on. Read the chapter thoroughly and understand what is being explained, otherwise what follows may be difficult to use. The names of the four basic symmetry operations – Rotation, Translation, Reflection and Glide Reflection – are the standard mathematical terms and are widely used. They are used here so that if you explore symmetry in other places, you will be comfortable with the terminology.

1.1 Rotation Symmetry

Definition
Rotation symmetry is the duplication by rotation of a figure around a central point.

Rotation symmetry is unique among the four symmetry operations because it creates symmetry around a point. The other three operations described later create symmetry along a line or across a plane. In this sense, rotation symmetry is a zero-dimensional (point) operation, not a one-dimensional (linear) or two-dimensional (planar) operation. However, as we will see in Chapter 2 and Chapter 3, it is entirely possible to use rotational motifs to create repeat patterns that are linear or planar.

In this basic example, the element, the lower case letterform f, is rotated through 180 degrees to create a motif. Note how the second step shows the original element in a light tint. This is to give visual emphasis to the rotated element, shown in a deeper shade of red. 180 degrees is the most common angle of rotation because it creates a motif with a simple symmetry. This form of rotation symmetry with just two elements is known as order 2 because the 360-degree rotation of a complete circle is divided into two equal parts, with 180 degrees between each element.

An example of rotation symmetry in nature is a snowflake, and in the manufactured world the spokes of a cartwheel.

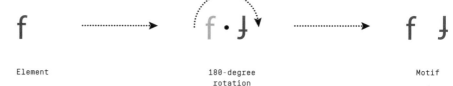

Element   180-degree rotation   Motif

Connected Elements
It is possible to create a motif with connected elements by placing the centre point of the rotation within or directly adjacent to the element.

Order 2 Variations

When making motifs with rotation symmetry, first it is essential to decide the position of the circle centre around which the element(s) will rotate. It can be in any position in relation to the element – above, below, left or right – and at any distance, near or far.

Here is a small selection of order 2 rotation symmetry motifs. There are many other possibilities.

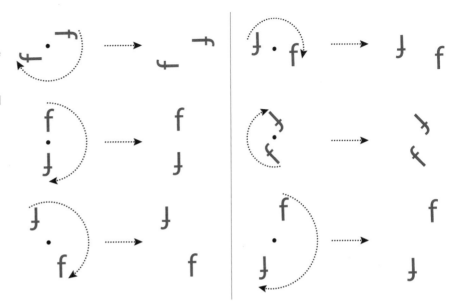

Orders 3, 4 and 5 Variations

The examples above are order 2 rotations. However, the 360 degrees of a complete rotation can be divided further, into 3, 4, 5, 6, 7, 8 and more divisions to infinity, and the centre point can be placed at any location in relation to the element.

Here are some examples of order 3, 4 and 5, which divide a circle of 360 degrees into 3, 4 or 5 equal parts. The number of the order describes by how much the 360 degrees has been equally divided. Thus, for example, order 3 means that 360 degrees has been divided into 3 equal parts of 120 degrees each.

The diversity of the patterns across the orders is remarkable. Remember, all the patterns were generated using the lower case letterform f.

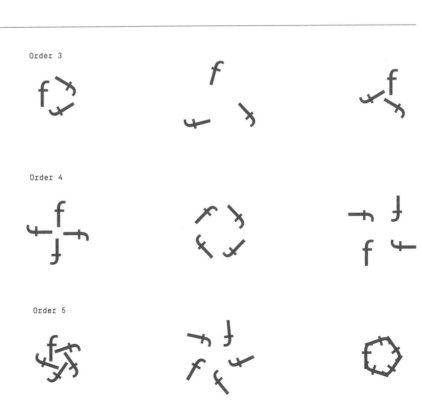

Order 3

Order 4

Order 5

Higher-order Variations
Orders 6 to 12 and above, which divide
a circle of 360 degrees into 6, 8 10, 12
and more equal parts. There is no limit
to the number of times that 360 degrees
can be divided.

Order 6

Order 8

Order 10

Order 12

Multi-order

1.2 Translation Symmetry

Definition
Translation symmetry is the movement of a figure (that is, an element, motif or meta-motif) a described distance in a described direction. The distance and angle between the figures remain constant and the figures neither rotate nor reflect.

q q

'Translation' is the term in Euclidean geometry for gliding a figure along a one-dimensional line, across a two-dimensional plane or through three-dimensional space. In some ways, translation symmetry is the most elementary of all symmetrical operations because it is the simple repetition of a figure along a line, so that all the figures are exactly alike. However, it can be a little puzzling to those who recall geometry lessons from their school days that defined symmetry to mean reflection, in the way that our two hands are mirror images of each other, or to mean rotation, like the arms of a starfish rotate around a central point. Where is the symmetry in translation symmetry? The answer is simply that symmetry can mean reflection or rotation, but it can also mean gliding. More formally, a definition of translation symmetry can be given as a figure sliding a described distance without rotating or reflecting.

The element, the lower case letterform q, is repeated by moving to the right. Translation symmetry is simply the movement of an element to another position, sometimes called a glide. If the element q was to be repeated again, the glide would continue along the same straight line and the distance between the elements would remain constant.

Examples of translation symmetry include a line of soliders standing at attention and a block of staples.

Variations

Translation symmetry may be considered a simple concept, yet the imaginative designer can use it to generate a vast number of subtle and creative patterns. Here are some basic variation concepts to consider.

Spacing

The distance between the elements can be anything from a little above zero to almost infinity. The smaller distances create their own chain link patterns that can be attractive.

q

Element

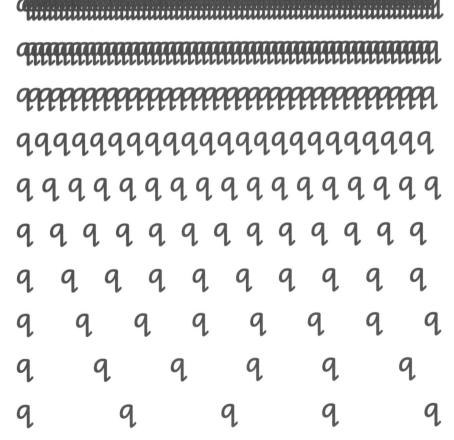

Rotation of the Element

Here, the element is rotated each time through an additional 45 degrees. At each angle the element looks different, offering new possibilities for translation symmetry patterns made from the element at that angle of rotation, as shown here.

Stepping between Elements

Instead of rotating the figure as in the image on the opposite page, it is also possible to step it; that is, to place a second element at an angle above or below the first. This is also an example of translation symmetry, but the direction of the glide will not be horizontal as before.

An interesting phenomenon of any translation technique, including stepping, is how different a repeat pattern can look when composed of an asymmetrical figure rotated through 180 degrees and viewed upside down. Three examples are shown here, each with two variations – each is the other turned through 180 degrees. The greater the asymmetry, the greater the apparent difference.

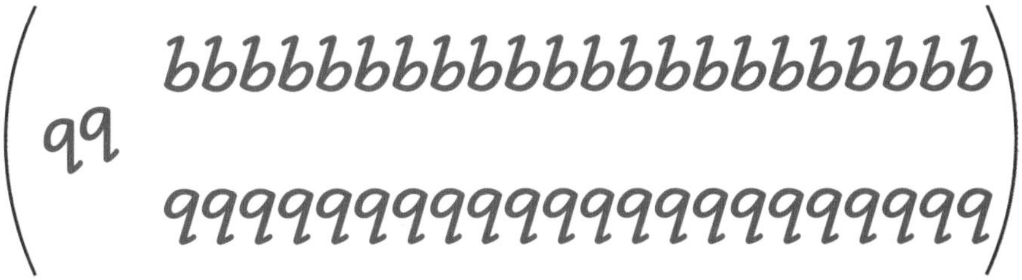

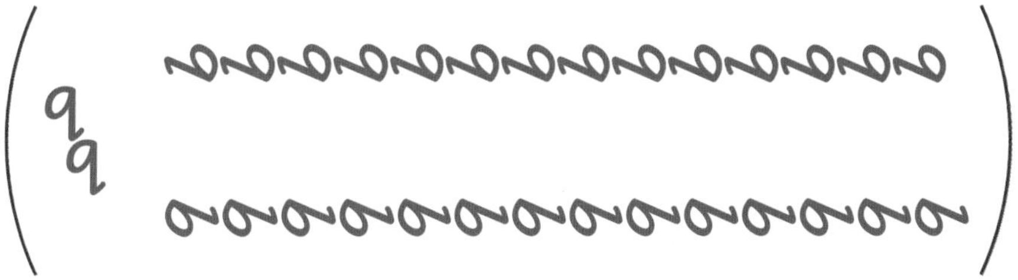

1.3 Reflection Symmetry

Definition
Reflection symmetry is when one half of a figure (that is, an element, motif or meta-motif) is the mirror image of the other half.

This is the operation most of us associate with symmetry and is the easiest to recognize. Perhaps this is because there are so many examples in nature. The ability to recognize reflection symmetry is almost subliminal; examples include the faces and bodies of most living creatures. It is also common in the manufactured world, from bottles to aircraft. Nevertheless, despite this great familiarity, there are many beautiful and little-known aspects of reflection symmetry to explore.

Reflection symmetry is the repetition of an element as a mirror image of itself. There is always a line between the two mirror-image elements along which the reflection is made.

In this basic example, the element, the lower case letterform h, is reflected along the axis of the red line to create the reflection symmetry motif. Note how the original element is repeated in the second step in a light tint of red. This is to give visual emphasis to its reflection, shown in a deeper shade of red.

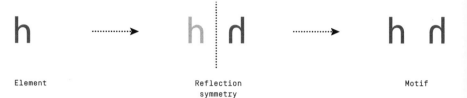

Element

Reflection
symmetry

Motif

Variations

Reflection symmetry is subject to fewer quirky variations than the other symmetry operations. This makes it both easier to use than the others, because the design perimeters are tighter, and more challenging, because innovation is more difficult. Nevertheless, it is the most common form of symmetry.

Spacing

In the centre of the top line of the illustration, the letterform h and its reflection are overlapped as compactly as possible, then they are gradually separated towards the left and right ends of the line. The separation continues to increase below the top line. Interesting motifs occur when the h and its reflection overlap, though it must always be remembered that there is still a relationship between them, even when the two halves of the motif are separated by a great distance.

Rotation of the Element

The top motif shows the h and its reflection in the standard position, the h standing upright. Below the top line, the h gradually rotates through 45-degree increments to create a series of interesting pictorial relationships between the two halves of the motif. The two halves can relate to each other at any angle.

Spacing + Rotation
When creating a motif, it is possible to combine the concept of spacing (see page 27) with that of rotation of the element (see page 22) to create an extraordinary number of very diverse motifs.

The top line of the illustration repeats the top line of the image on page 31. The seven rows under this line show the element and its reflection progressively rotating through 45-degree increments, gradually stretching apart towards the left and right ends of each row. Only lack of space in the book prevents the inclusion of more motifs; with this simple combination of techniques, the number of motifs generated becomes almost overwhelming.

1.4 Glide Reflection Symmetry

Definition

Glide Reflection symmetry combines two symmetry operations. First, a translation symmetry operation is made, followed by a reflection symmetry operation in the same direction as the translation.

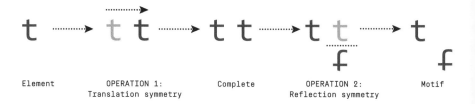

| Element | OPERATION 1: Translation symmetry | Complete | OPERATION 2: Reflection symmetry | Motif |

Glide Reflection symmetry is unique among the four symmetry operations described in this chapter because it combines two operations. For this reason, it is the most complex and the least used of the four. However, when understood it is no more complex than the other operations, though perhaps less intuitive to use and more difficult to visualize. This subtlety can create very sophisticated repeat patterns.

Note that the order of the two operations can be reversed to achieve the same final effect. Note also that glide reflection does not create the same motif as rotation symmetry. The similarity of appearance means that it is sometimes mistakenly referred to as rotation symmetry. A good visual analogy is to think of left and right foot imprints created when you walk in sand – the line of footprints normally displays glide reflection symmetry.

In this basic example, the element, the lower case letterform t, is first translated, then the new element is reflected along a line parallel to the line of the translation. The second element is removed, to leave a motif of the first and third elements only.

Variations

The opportunities for creating a long series of diverse motifs are less with glide reflection symmetry than with the three other symmetry operations. Relating just two elements together this way offers a relatively limited number of opportunities, though the repeat patterns the operation helps to create are often pleasingly enigmatic.

Relative Proportions of Translation and Reflection

Glide Reflection consists of two symmetry operations, translation and reflection. The proportionate distance length of each operation is variable and also relative to the other operation. Thus, the distance length of one operation could be less, the same or greater than the distance length of the other operation.

In the top example, the reflection distance remains the same, while the translation distance progressively increases.

In the middle example, the translation distance remains the same, while the reflection distance progressively increases.

In the bottom example, both the translation and the reflection distances increase proportionately.

1.4 Glide Reflection Symmetry

Rotation of the Element
As with the other three symmetry operations in this chapter, surprising relationships occur between the two elements when they are rotated. With glide reflection, the relations can be so extreme that it is sometimes difficult to recognize a form of symmetry at work within a motif.

Shown here are four examples of a rotated element in which the translation distance is progressively increased.

Two examples of a rotated element in which the reflection distance is progressively increased.

Three examples of a rotated element in which both the translation and reflection distances are progressively increased.

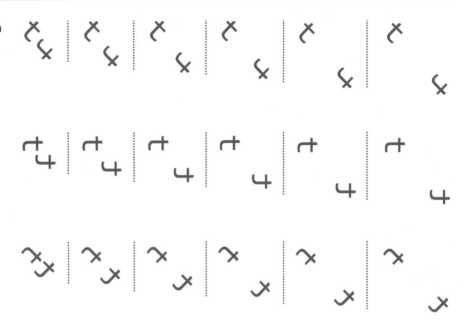

2. Linear Symmetry

Linear symmetry is a one-dimensional symmetry operation made along a straight line. Examples of common applications for linear symmetry might include an architectural frieze, a decorative border on a printed page or a line of bird tracks in the snow. It should not be confused with the similarly named line or lines of symmetry, which refer to the line(s) dividing the two mirror-image halves of a Reflection symmetry motif.

There are seven linear symmetry operations, all of which use one or more of the four symmetry operations described in the previous chapter, namely Rotation, Translation, Reflection and Glide Reflection. Since Rotation symmetry is a zero-dimensional symmetry operation around a point, not a one-dimensional symmetry operation along a line, it cannot be discussed in this chapter. However, as we will see, though Rotation symmetry cannot be performed as a stand-alone operation to create linear symmetry, it can be combined with the other three operations to create linear symmetry patterns.

2.1 Translation

Linear translation symmetry is the most basic of the seven linear symmetry operations. It is simply the repetition of an element, motif or meta-motif in a straight line, with equal spacing and without rotating or reflecting the figure.

In this basic example, the upper case letterform F is repeated in a straight line using the translation symmetry operation.

Element   Translation   Linear translation symmetry
                 symmetry
                 operation

Spacing
The figure can be repeated along the line at any interval. However, to be a repeat pattern and to be symmetrical, the interval must remain constant.

FFFFFFFFFFFFFFFFFFFFFFFFFF

F F F F F F F F F F F F F F F F F

F F F F F F F F

Orientation of the Element
The element can be rotated through any number of degrees, then repeated in a straight line with any spacing.

Multiple Elements
Any number of elements can be arranged to create a motif or mega-motif, which can be repeated in a straight line, with any spacing. Using even the simplest element, there are a huge number of possibilities.

2.2 Translation + Vertical Reflection

Translation + Vertical Reflection is more commonly known as mirror reflection. It can be compared to holding up your two hands and seeing how each is the mirror reflection of the other. However, in its full form this symmetry operation assumes an infinite number of hands in a straight line – thumb to thumb and little finger to little finger – not just a pair.

In this basic example, the upper case letterform Q is reflected along a vertical axis to create a reflection of itself. This reflection is then itself mirrored to create a copy of the initial element. In this way, each element in the line is the reflection of the elements to either side.

Element

Reflection
symmetry
operation

Linear vertical reflection symmetry

Spacing
It is possible to create the first line of reflection at any distance from the element, from almost zero to infinity, even within the element itself. These motifs can then be repeated along the line at any consistent distance from each other, from almost zero to infinity. In this way, there are two spacing variables that can affect the linear pattern. The selection here shows a few possibilities.

Orientation of the Element

The element Q can be presented at any angle through a full 360-degree rotation, though the line of reflection will always be along a vertical axis. The spacing of these motifs is a second variable.

Multiple Elements

The single element Q can be used any number of times to create a motif, which can then be reflected. Here, in the first example, two Qs are reflected and in the second example, three are reflected. By experimenting with spacing, orientation and multiple elements, a vast number of possibilities for creating repeat patterns will quickly emerge.

2.3 Translation + 180-degree Rotation

Two symmetry operations combine to create a motif. First, the element is repeated to the side (translation), then rotated through 180 degrees (rotation). This motif is then repeated along a line. Each element in the line is rotated through 180 degrees compared with the elements on either side. This symmetry operation may appear to be a simple rotation without translation, but the combination of the two operations create linear symmetry, not rotation symmetry.

The upper case letterform P is first translated and then rotated through 180 degrees. These two symmetry operations combine to create a motif that is then repeated along a line.

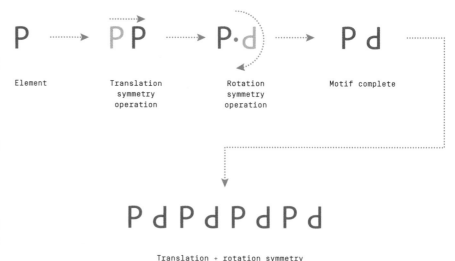

P ·······▶ PP̄ ·······▶ P·d ·······▶ P d

Element   Translation   Rotation   Motif complete
          symmetry   symmetry
          operation   operation

P d P d P d P d

Translation + rotation symmetry

Spacing

While the translation symmetry operations can be performed at any distance from almost zero to infinity, the rotation operation is not a variable. However, the motifs can be placed at any distance from each other, so this creates a second variable. When the two variables are performed, many different repeat patterns can be created.

PdPdPdPdPdPdPdPdPdPdPdPdPdPdPdPdPdPdPd

PdPdPdPdPdPdPdPdPdPdPdPdPdPdPdPdPdPdPdPd

PdPdPdPdPdPdPdPdPdPdPdPdPdPdPdPdPdPdPdPd

PdPdPdPdPdPdPdPdPdPdPdPd

P d P d P d P d P d P d P d P

Orientation of the Element

The element P can be presented at any angle through a full 360-degree rotation, though the translation must always be in the same direction. The spacing of these motifs is a second variable.

Multiple Elements

The single element P can be used any number of times to create a motif, which can then be translated and rotated. In the first and second examples here, two Ps are combined; in the third example, four are stacked. By experimenting with spacing, orientation and multiple elements, a vast number of possibilities for creating repeat patterns will quickly emerge.

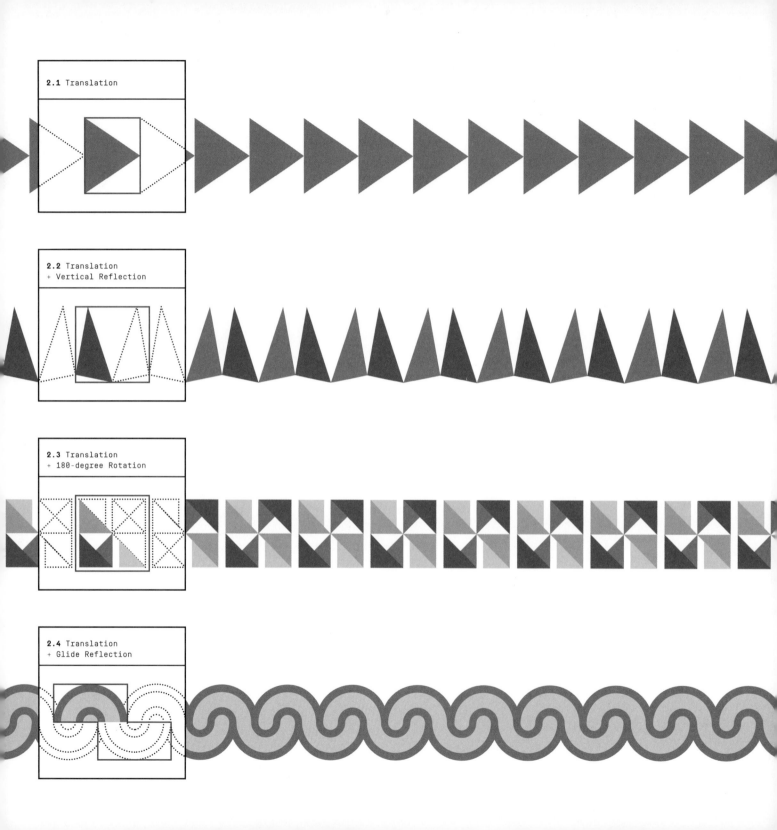

2.1 Translation

2.2 Translation
+ Vertical Reflection

2.3 Translation
+ 180-degree Rotation

2.4 Translation
+ Glide Reflection

2.5 Horizontal Reflection

2.6 Vertical Reflection + Translation + Horizontal Reflection + 180-degree Rotation

2.7 Translation + Vertical Reflection + 180-degree Rotation + Vertical Reflection

2.4 Translation + Glide Reflection

The construction of the motif may at first be a little awkward to grasp fully, but can be easily understood by imagining a line of footprints in the sand. The footprints analogy was used in Chapter 1 as an example of glide reflection, but when the symmetry operation is linear, the same operation is known as Translation + Glide Reflection. Note how the symmetry operation creates upper and lower elements (not elements in a single line), which combine to make a linear symmetry pattern of greater visual complexity than seen previously.

In this basic example, the upper case letterform G is first repeated by translation, then that repetition is reflected along a horizontal axis. In the example shown here, the horizontal axis is below the letter G, but it could also have been above it. The intermediary translation stage is removed, to leave a final motif of two elements.

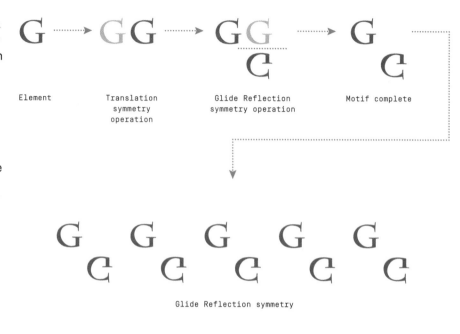

Element — Translation symmetry operation — Glide Reflection symmetry operation — Motif complete

Glide Reflection symmetry

Spacing

Both the distance moved to the side during the translation symmetry operation and the placement of the horizontal line of reflection relative to the translated element are variable. One or both can have a separation from the previous element anywhere between almost zero and infinity. The examples here show a selection of possibilities.

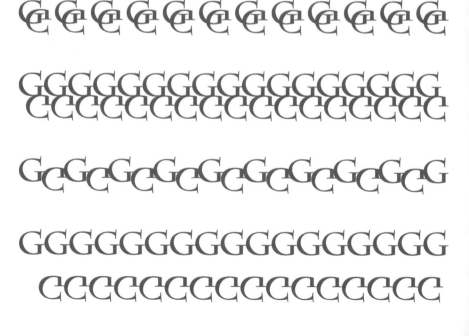

Orientation of the Element

The element G can be presented at any angle through to a full 360-degree rotation, though the translation must always be in the same direction and the line of reflection must always be along the line of travel. The spacing between the motifs can be anything between almost zero and infinity.

Multiple Elements

The single element G can be used any number of times to create a motif, which can then be translated and reflected. In this example, two Gs are combined. If the element is repeated a large number of times, there is a danger of the final motif becoming visually too complex, so care must be taken when using this symmetry operation that it does not create an incoherent pattern. By experimenting with spacing, orientation and multiple elements, a vast number of possibilities for creating repeat patterns will quickly emerge.

2.5 Horizontal Reflection

This is one of the simplest and most intuitive symmetry operations. It is an operation that creates clean and simple repeat patterns that are easy to understand. Remember, though, that while the reflection is in a vertical direction, the line of reflection is horizontal, hence the name of the operation.

In this basic example, the upper case letterform J is reflected across a horizontal line of reflection to create a mirror-image motif that pairs together two elements. The horizontal line could be below the element (as shown here) or above, or even at some point within the element. The linear symmetry is created when the motif is repeated a consistent distance apart in the same direction as the horizontal line of reflection.

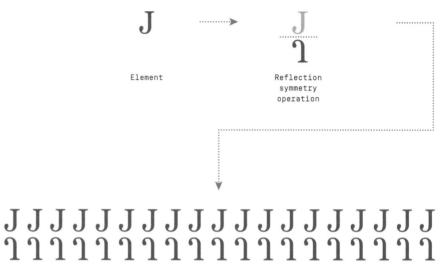

Element

Reflection symmetry operation

Linear horizontal reflection symmetry

Spacing
The horizontal line across which the element is reflected can be placed anywhere within the element, or above or below it. This leads to a series of relatively simple but surprisingly diverse motifs. The horizontal separation of the motifs can be anything between almost zero to infinity.

Orientation of the Element

The element J can be presented at any angle through to a full 360-degree rotation, though the line of reflection must always remain horizontal and the line of repeated motifs must extend in the same direction as that line.

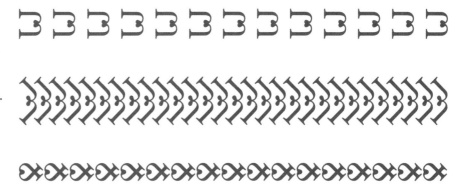

Multiple Elements

The motif created before it is reflected can have any number of elements. The first of the two examples here shows three Js reflected to create a motif of six Js. The second example is more complex because there are two horizontal reflections, doubling two Js to four and then again to a stack of eight. The symmetry is still linear symmetry, but if the pattern was reflected again and perhaps again to increase its height, it would become an example of planar symmetry. It's an interesting point of discussion: when does linear symmetry become planar symmetry? Perhaps there is no single or useful answer!

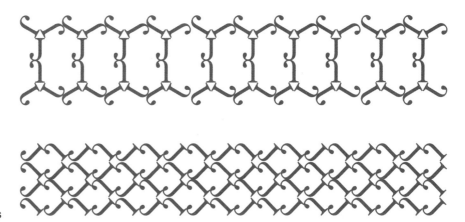

2.6 Vertical Reflection + Translation + Horizontal Reflection + 180-degree Rotation

The title of this form of linear symmetry is accurate, but difficult to absorb or remember. In simple terms, a motif is made of a block of four elements, each of which is a reflection of its neighbours to the left or right and above or below. The formality of the symmetry tends to create repeat patterns that are also formal.

In this basic example, the upper case letterform L is taken through three separate symmetry operations. First, the element is reflected vertically. Second, the primary element is reflected horizontally. Third, the primary element is rotated through 180 degrees, with the point of rotation at the midpoint of the three elements. The result is a motif grid of four elements, each of which is a reflection of its neighbours. This motif can then be repeated along a line to create a repeat pattern. The written description of the symmetry operations is comparatively lengthy, but the visual result is easy to understand.

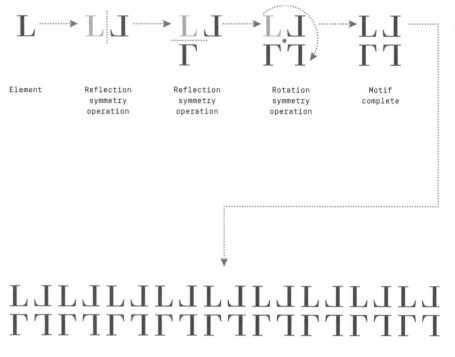

Element   Reflection symmetry operation   Reflection symmetry operation   Rotation symmetry operation   Motif complete

Reflection + reflection + rotation symmetry

Spacing

The three separate symmetry operations provide a succession of opportunities to create an extensive set of motifs from the same element, though all with a sense of order and balance created by the two reflection operations. The examples here show some of the possibilities when the horizontal and vertical lines of reflection are moved up and down and left and right, relative to the element and to each other.

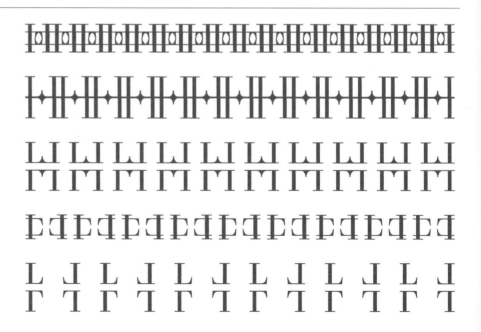

Orientation of the Element

Even when the element is rotated to an unlikely angle and taken through the three symmetry operations, the repeat patterns are still surprisingly coherent. You could take it as a design challenge to try to create a wild and expressive pattern using this grid repeat.

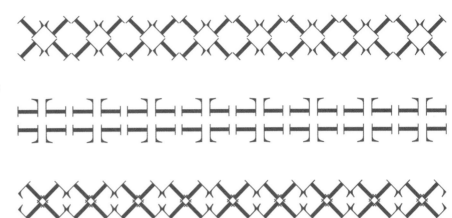

Multiple Elements

The stability of this form of linear symmetry is evident even when multiple elements are used. The two examples here show the extremes of the symmetry operations. The first example shows two elements placed precisely together to create a formal repeat. The second example shows four elements placed randomly together. However, when taken through the sequence of three symmetry operations, even this random composition acquires a pleasing degree of order.

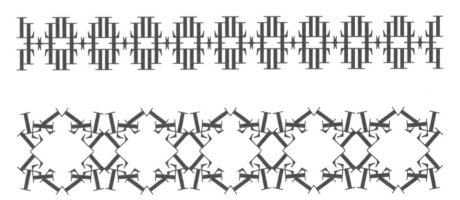

2.7 Translation + Vertical Reflection + 180-degree Rotation + Vertical Reflection

This is the only example of linear symmetry that has a motif consisting of a single line of four elements. The motif can be described precisely, but when expanded into a line of repeats, the pattern can be described in a many different ways, depending on which element is chosen to begin the description. The repeat patterns are subtle and complex.

In this basic example, the upper case letterform R is taken through three symmetry operations, each performed along the same horizontal line. First, the element is reflected along a vertical line, perpendicular to a line of translation. Second, the new element is rotated through 180 degrees. Third, the new element is again reflected along a vertical line, perpendicular to the line of translation. The line of four elements combine to create a complex motif, which is then expanded to create a repeat pattern.

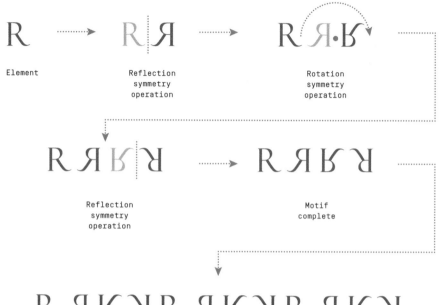

Element

Reflection
symmetry
operation

Rotation
symmetry
operation

Reflection
symmetry
operation

Motif
complete

Reflection + rotation + reflection symmetry

Spacing
The complex construction of the motif permits many variations in the way that the elements are spaced, allowing the creation of repeat patterns that are both conventional and eccentric.

Orientation of the Element

The element R can be presented at any angle through to a full 360-degree rotation, which when taken through the succession of symmetry operations will create a pleasing diversity of repeat patterns. Note that the pattern will repeat every four elements, beginning the count at any element.

Multiple Elements

A complex succession of symmetry operations can quickly create an incoherent visual pattern of little interest. Care in the distribution of multiple elements will help ensure that what you design will hold a viewer's attention. Even subtle adjustments in how the elements relate and where the lines of reflection are located can have a major impact on how a repeat pattern looks, so be prepared to experiment as much as time permits.

3. Planar Symmetry

Planar symmetry is symmetry on a two-dimensional plane. It is created when symmetry operations are made both across and down a two-dimensional plane (a flat surface), thus covering the surface. It is by far the most common form of pattern making. Indeed, it is so common in our everyday lives that patterns created through planar symmetry often go unnoticed. They occur at all scales, from the crisscross of threads in a woven or knitted fabric, to the arrangement of squares on a chess board, to the layout of seats in a theatre and the grid of streets in a modern city.

Most planar symmetry repeat patterns are square or rectangular grids. This form of 90-degree geometry is so common as to be made almost without thought of possible alternatives and can fairly be considered a design cliché. There are many practical advantages to making 90-degree corners, but the alternatives of 60-degree and 120-degree geometries to create triangular and hexagonal symmetry patterns should not be dismissed without study. This chapter describes these alternative geometries. If you are unfamiliar with them, they are well worth special attention. They are no more difficult to create than patterns that use 90-degree geometry, but our familiarity with 90-degree geometry can make patterns made with alternative geometries seem uncomfortably strange, when they are simply different.

Many of the cells used in planar symmetry operations can be used as the basis of tiling patterns, which are explained in the next chapter. For more information about cells and tiles, see pages 14–15.

3.1 Translation

Translation symmetry on the plane is the most straightforward of all symmetry operations. It is simply the placing of an element or motif inside a cell, and repeating that cell both horizontally and vertically across the plane to create a regular grid. The simplicity of this symmetry operation can be deceptive, though, and many repeat patterns of great subtlety can be created with it.

In this basic example, the element, the lower case letterform a, is placed inside a square cell, shown with a red border. The cells are then repeated both horizontally and vertically across the plane, without spaces in between. When the red cells are removed, the repeat pattern is a regular grid of elements (of course, the red cell walls could remain as part of the repeat pattern).

Element

Cell

Cell + element

Complete

Cell Size
In the two examples shown here, the element a is the same size, but the cells are different sizes. The effect is to first crowd the elements together and then to separate them widely. Thus, by changing the size of the cell relative to the size of the element, the spacing between the elements can be controlled and the proportions of a repeat pattern can be precisely determined.

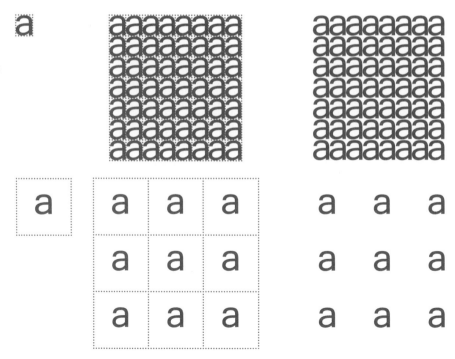

Cell Shape

Square cells will easily fit together without spaces, and so will rectangles. The two examples here show the element inside a vertical-format rectangle and then inside a horizontal-format rectangle. The effect is to first create rows of elements and then to create columns. By changing the proportions of a rectangular cell, the spacing of the rows and columns can be controlled. The cells can be made larger, relative to the element, thus increasing the spaces between the elements (see opposite page).

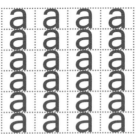

Direction of Translation

We have previously seen translation symmetry create repeat patterns with neat rows and columns of elements at 90 degrees to each other. However, it is also possible to tile a surface by offsetting the cells, commonly called a half-drop repeat. The first example shows the offsetting of alternate rows of cells and the second shows the offsetting of alternate columns. Note how the two directions of translation are not at 90 degrees to each other. By changing the cell size and the cell shape (discussed above), the angle between the two directions of translation will become different.

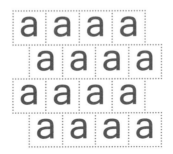
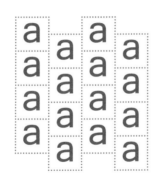
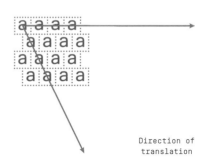

Direction of translation

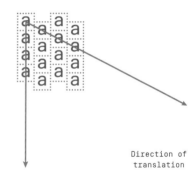

Direction of translation

3.2 Glide Reflection

Glide Reflection symmetry is the most enigmatic of the four basic symmetry operations described in Chapter 1. This is because it is a two-step operation, with the middle (connecting) step removed, leaving a motif of two seemingly disconnected elements. The result of this two-step operation is to create repeat patterns that are more sophisticated than simpler rotation and reflection patterns.

In this basic example, the element, the lower case letterform b, is taken through two symmetry operations. First, it performs a vertical glide downwards, then it is reflected to the side along a vertical line of reflection. The middle step is removed and the first and last elements combine to create a motif that is placed in a cell. The cells are then repeated across the plane to create a repeat pattern.

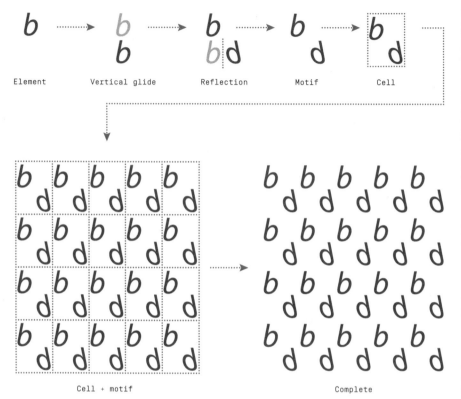

Spacing

The five examples here show a selection of ways in which the two symmetry operations can be expanded or contracted, so that the two elements in the motif have a different spatial relationship with each other. In turn, this will affect the proportions of a rectangular cell. Some motifs are relatively conventional, but others are not, which creates unusual secondary relationships between the elements of different cells.

Cell Shape

The conventional shape for the cell is a square or rectangle, but any quadrilateral with opposite sides that are parallel – that is, a rhombus or a parallelogram – will also tile without spaces. The use of these skewed cells can help create extreme alignments of the elements that are not possible with squares and rectangles.

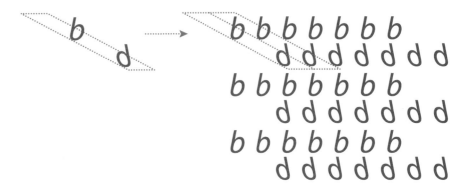

3.1 Translation

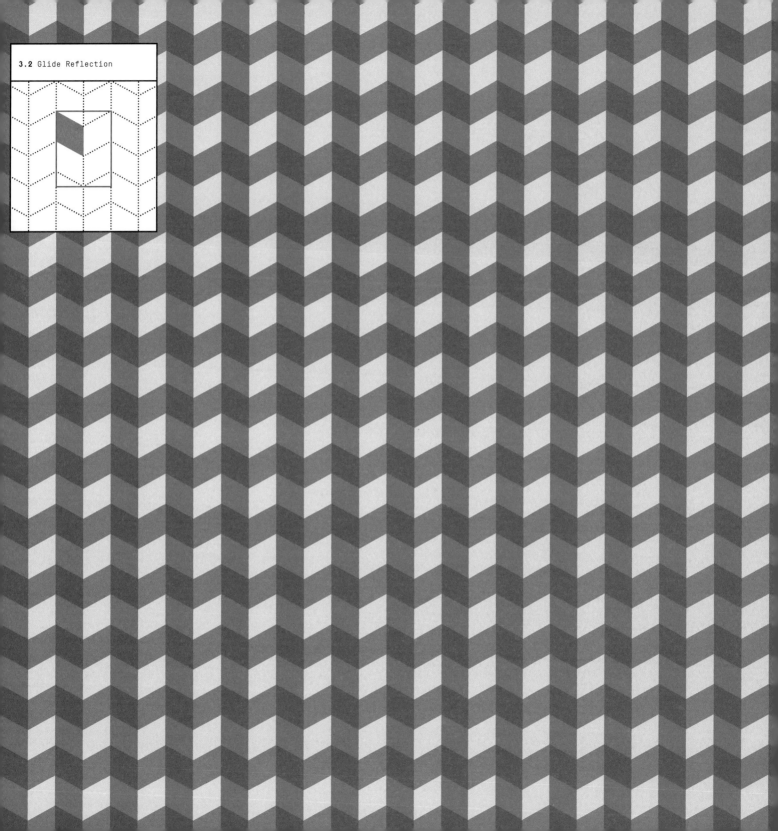

3.2 Glide Reflection

3.3 Double Reflection

At first glance, double reflection symmetry can seem to involve a lot of unnecessary explanation. However, a deeper understanding will reveal the hidden principle behind what seems like a simple effect. When this principle is understood, it makes the symmetry operation easier to apply.

In this basic example, the element we are using for the first time is a symmetrical lower case letterform: v. Using the same typeface, other letters could include i, l, o, w and x. The v is divided in half, so that the element is just one angled straight line. This element is reflected first to the left and then to the right to create a motif. This double reflection can then be repeated along a line and the lines arranged in rows to create planar symmetry.

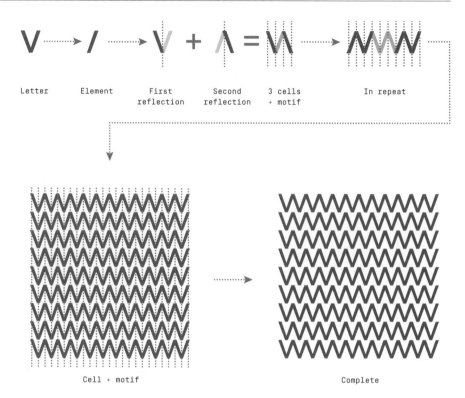

| Letter | Element | First reflection | Second reflection | 3 cells + motif | In repeat |

Cell + motif   Complete

Cell Size

The cell can be tight to the element so that all the elements join up in a continuous ribbon, or the cell can grow so that there are spaces between the elements. The examples here show the gradual separation of the elements.

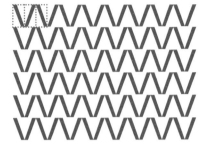

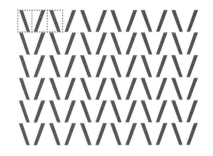

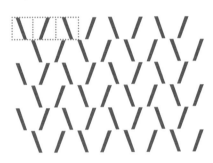

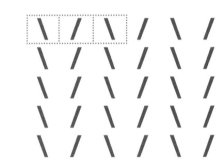

Asymmetrical Elements

The elements need not be a simple symmetrical form, such as the letter v on the opposite page, which has a vertical line of symmetry. The element can also have a horizontal line of symmetry, such as the C seen here, or be asymmetrical, like the R. The rows can be tightly stacked or have spaces between them. Note that in the R repeat, the different rows are offset to create a more complex pattern.

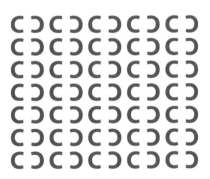

3.4 Reflection + Parallel Glide Reflection

This is one of the planar symmetry operations that naturally creates spaces in the cell, making it ideal for creating uncluttered repeats. It is even possible to introduce a second, different repeat pattern into the spaces, so that the two patterns coexist on the same plane.

In this basic example, the element, the lower case letterform y, is first reflected, then the newly created second element translates (glides) downwards, before being reflected in the direction of the first reflection to create the third element. The fourth element is a reflection of the third element. The final motif thus has four elements in a staggered arrangement, the lower pair of elements being identical to the upper pair. This sequence of manoeuvres is simple to grasp visually.

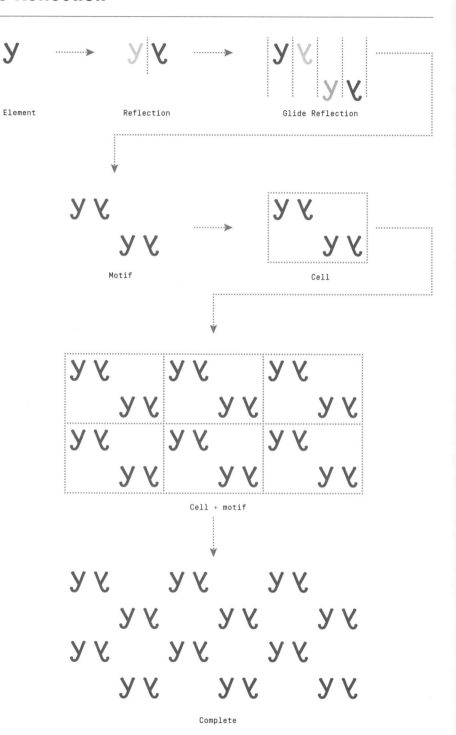

Element

Reflection

Glide Reflection

Motif

Cell

Cell + motif

Complete

Spacing

The three reflection operations and one translation operation can all be compressed or expanded so that the final cell is small or large, as required. The cells can also overlap to further compress the repeat pattern.

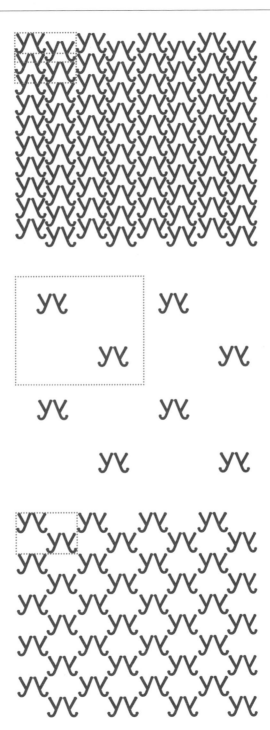

3.3 Double Reflection

3.4 Reflection
+ Parallel Glide Reflection

3.5 180-degree Rotation

The 180-degree rotation symmetry operation is one of the simplest and most intuitive of all the planar symmetry operations. However, as simple as they are, the cells can be placed in an intriguing series of tiling arrangements to create repeat patterns that are interesting and different from each other. Consider how this symmetry operation differs from the similar-looking Double Reflection symmetry operation on pages 64–65.

In this basic example, the element, the lower case letterform r, is rotated through 180 degrees to create a second element. These two elements create the motif. The boundary of the cell wall can be tight to the motif or separated from it. What a refreshingly simple description!

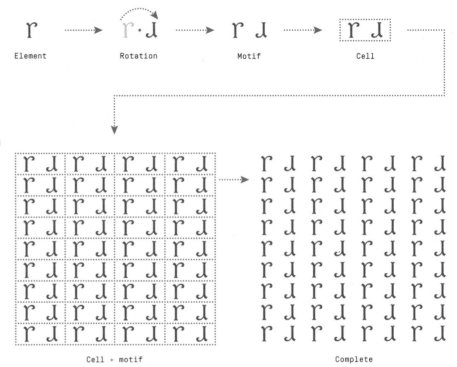

Element   Rotation   Motif   Cell

Cell + motif

Complete

Direction of Rotation

While it is common and entirely normal to rotate the element to the right, it may also be rotated downwards, so that the repeat pattern extends down as a column, not across as a row. It may also be rotated upwards or to the left, though these orientations would not create original motifs, just reflections of existing ones.

Tiling the Cells

Look very closely at the four examples here. The first two are very similar, but the different ways in which the cells stack on top of each other results in a difference in how the rows of cells relate. The subtlety is both fascinating and instructive. The final example moves each row of cells half a cell to the right, like a wall of bricks, creating a different column alignment of the elements.

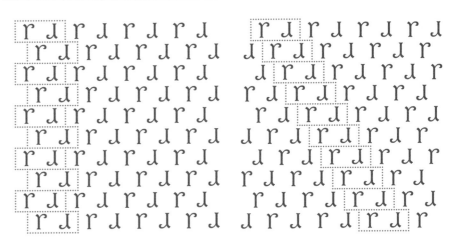

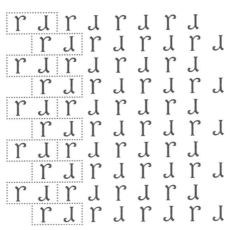

3.6 Reflection + Perpendicular Glide Reflection

This is another planar symmetry operation which, like Reflection + Parallel Glide Reflection (page 66), has the potential to create space within the repeat. The sequence of operations creates a motif of four elements that should be compared with Reflection + Parallel Glide Reflection. The differences are instructive and together they will generate many different possibilities for making repeat patterns.

In this basic example, the element, the lower case letterform t, is first reflected. Then, perpendicular to the line of the reflection, a glide reflection operation is performed on the first element. Finally, the new third element is reflected along the same line as the first reflection. The motif retains all four elements. The cell, if it excludes the spaces to the top right and bottom left of the motif, will be an unusual configuration of two connected rectangles that will still tile without spaces.

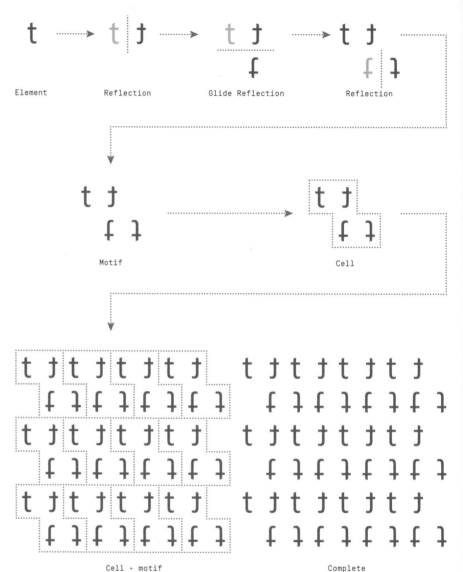

Cell Shape

The cell shape, whether it is made of a simple single rectangle, as seen here, or connected rectangles, as seen on the opposite page, can expand or shrink to enlarge or tighten the repeat pattern. These operations can be made to feature or almost eliminate the spaces that appear in the motif. The two examples here show the cell contracting.

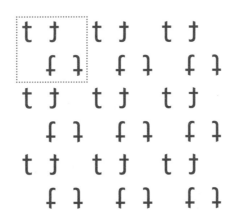
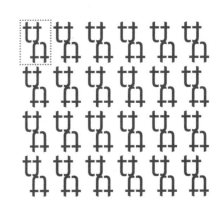

One Unique Cell or Many Different Cells?

This is a good moment to consider what makes a cell. In a four-element motif like this one, the cell is constructed one way in the basic example above, but when cells are combined in a grid to create a repeat pattern, other possible cells become apparent.

The examples here all show the same repeat pattern, but the cells are different. Some repeat patterns have a great many possible cells and these different cells are all of equal merit. On the same repeat pattern, some cells will be rectangular, others will be parallelograms or L-shaped, and if the geometry uses angles of 120, 60 or 30 degrees, cells can also be triangular or hexagonal … and more. Can you find any non-rectangular cells in the repeat patterns here? There are many!

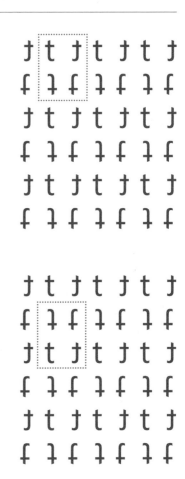

3.5 180-degree Rotation

3.5 180-degree Rotation

3.5 180-degree Rotation

3.6 Reflection +
Perpendicular Glide
Reflection

3.7 Two Perpendicular Glide Reflections

Like Reflection + Parallel Glide Reflection (page 66), this planar symmetry operation features two glide reflections, but this time progresses in a downwards direction instead of horizontally. The effect is to realign the four elements of the motif from the horizontal to the vertical and thus create new possibilities for repeat patterns. As before, the symmetry operations generate spaces within the motif and the rectangular cell.

In this basic example, the element, the lower case letterform q, first undergoes a glide reflection to create a second element. This new element is then rotated downwards through 180 degrees to create a third element. A fourth element is generated when the third element undergoes another glide reflection, but in the reverse direction to the first glide reflection. This creates an unusual motif that is predominantly vertical, though it could be rotated to the horizontal. The cell contains four elements and also four spaces, which creates a sparse repeat pattern.

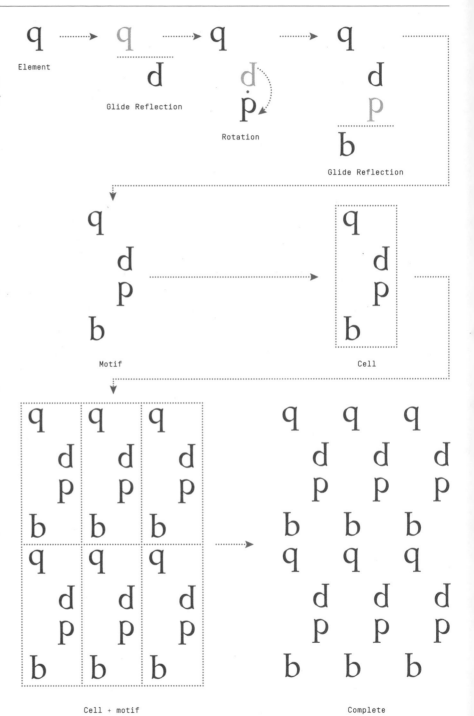

Cell Shape

The four elements in the cell can be compressed to eliminate the four spaces, thus creating a tall, thin cell. The repeat pattern will look very different if the grid is rotated through 90 degrees. This, of course, is true for any repeat pattern, but is particularly noteworthy here; the two patterns seem different, but are actually the same.

q q q q q q q
d d d d d d d
p p p p p p p
b b b b b b b
q q q q q q q
d d d d d d d
p p p p p p p
b b b b b b b

3.8 90-degree Reflections around a Point

The arrangement of reflections around a central point gives this sequence of symmetry operations the potential to create attractive repeat patterns using almost any element, however unpromising it may initially seem. The ease with which successful designs can be created perhaps also makes it difficult to create something exceptional.

In this basic example, the element, the lower case letterform h, is taken through a sequence of three 90-degree reflections around the central point where the reflection axes meet, so that each of the four elements is the reflection of its neighbours to either side. The final motif will sit neatly in a rectangular cell, which can then be repeated to create a grid.

Note that once the planar repeat has been made, the cell that defines the motif to be repeated can be placed in many positions on the grid. See pages 110–112 for a fuller explanation. Note also the similarity of the operation to Reflection + Perpendicular Glide Reflection on page 72. However, the latter includes a glide reflection, whereas the operation here is a simple 4-fold reflection around a point, considerably simplifying the motif.

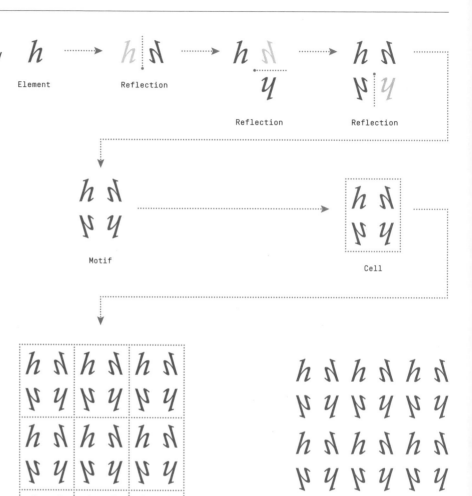

Orientation of the Element

Different orientations of an element will create surprisingly different repeat patterns, so time taken to explore the potential of even the plainest of elements will be well rewarded. When combined with the shape of the cell and the spacing between them, both discussed elsewhere in this chapter, this form of planar symmetry becomes versatile and fun to use.

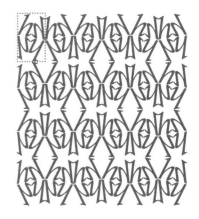

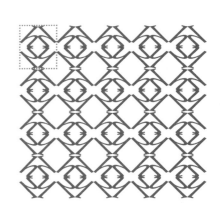

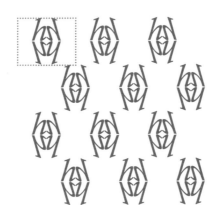

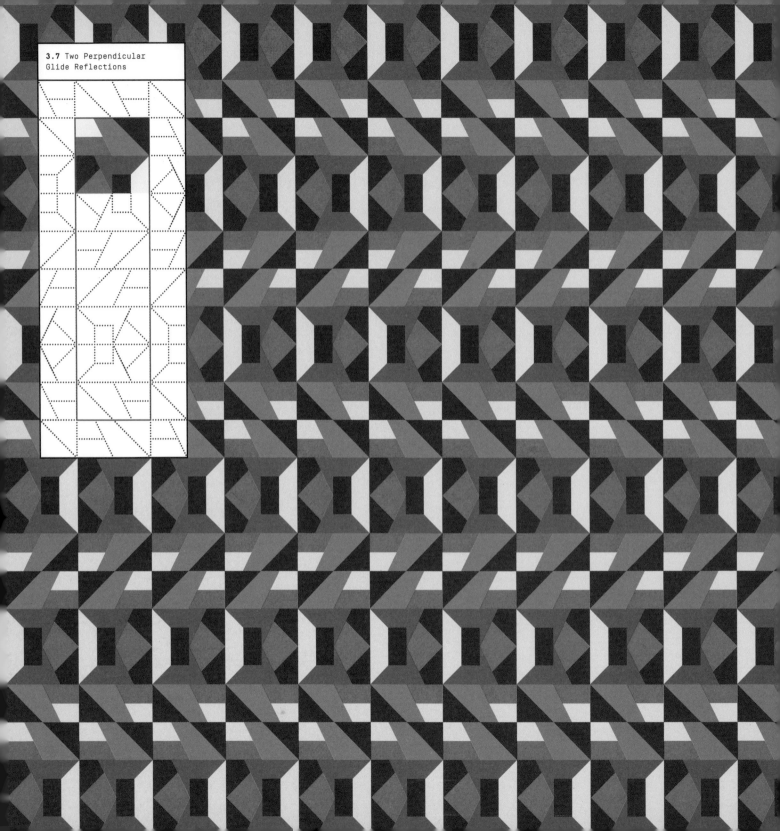

3.7 Two Perpendicular
Glide Reflections

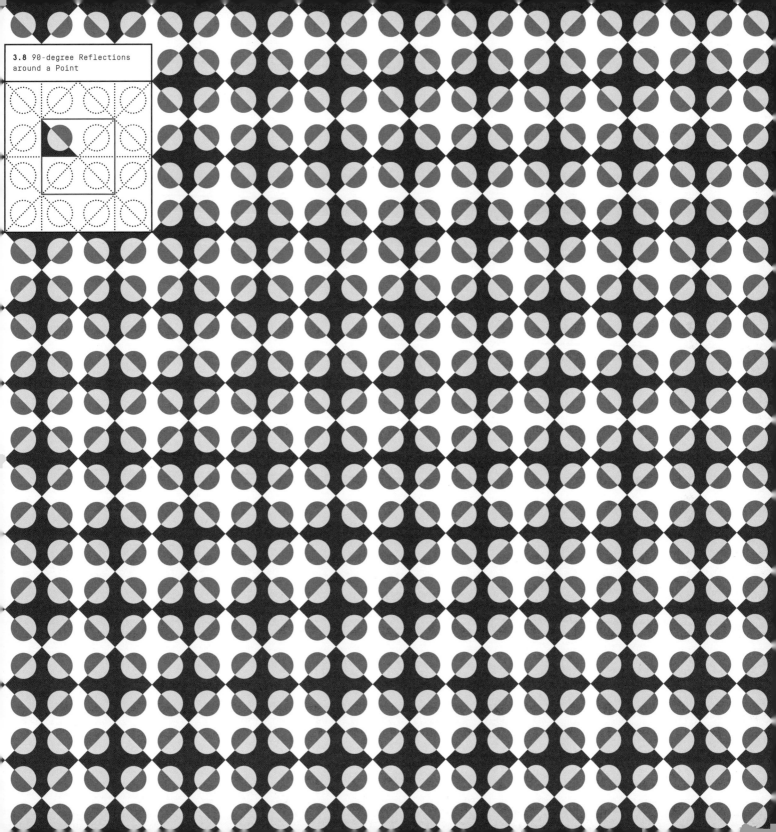

3.8 90-degree Reflections around a Point

3.9 Reflection + Rotation + Reflection + Perpendicular Reflection

This is the most complex of the 90-degree forms of planar symmetry. It consists of eight elements and has the potential to create repeat patterns of great complexity. It is similar to the previous form of symmetry, so to help a more direct comparison between the two, the same element (the lower case letterform h) has been used again here.

In this basic example, the element is first reflected, then both elements are rotated through 180 degrees in the same direction as the reflection. Finally, these four elements are reflected perpendicularly to the previous symmetry operations to create a motif of eight elements. The motif will always create a cell with a conventional rectangular format.

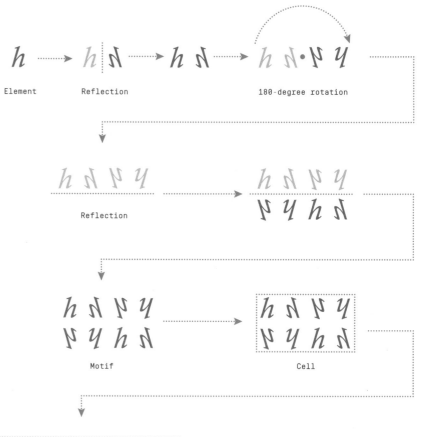

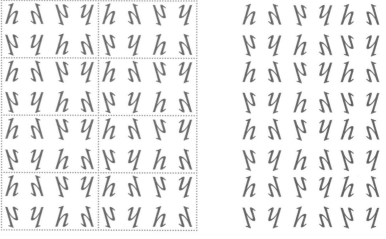

Cell + motif

Complete

Orientation of the Element

The element can be orientated at different angles to create surprisingly different patterns. The sequence of symmetry operations performed means that many of the repeat patterns will have a pleasingly staggered or negative–positive appearance, which are difficult to achieve with other forms of planar symmetry.

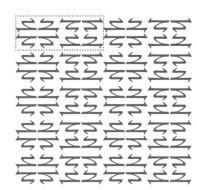

3.10 Three 120-degree Rotations

This is the first of a number of planar symmetry forms that use 120-, 60- or 30-degree geometries. They are known as order 3, order 6 and order 12 rotations because they divide a full rotation of 360 degrees into three, six and twelve parts. This alternative way of dividing the plane generates multiples of three or six elements that create triangular or hexagonal cells, instead of the more familiar 180-, 90- or 45-degree geometry that generates multiples of two or four elements and creates quadrilateral cells. All 17 forms of planar symmetry use one or other of these two systems. They never combine (unless different motifs are layered on the same plane).

In this basic example, the element, the lower case letterform d, is rotated 120 degrees around a point to create a second element, then rotated again through a further 120 degrees to create a third element, thus dividing a full rotation of 360 degrees into three parts with three elements to create an order 3 rotation. The motif of three elements creates a triangular cell.

To develop the repeat pattern, each corner of the triangular cell is used as a point around which three 120-degree rotations are made. Thus, the repeat pattern consists of two different points of rotation; at the centre of each cell and at the corners of each cell. The triangular grid of cells can expand in any and all directions across the plane. Note how the triangular voids are actually hexagonal, since they are bordered by six elements, not three.

Element   120-degree   Motif   Cell
           rotation

Cell + motif

Complete

Orientation of the Element

The first point of rotation (at the centre of the cell) can be placed anywhere around or inside the element. Similarly, the second point of rotation (at the corners of the cells) can be anywhere, depending on the orientation and size of the cell relative to the three elements. The example here shows the point of rotation in a different place from the three elements, compared with the point of rotation shown in the basic example on the opposite page. The result, of course, is a repeat pattern with new characteristics.

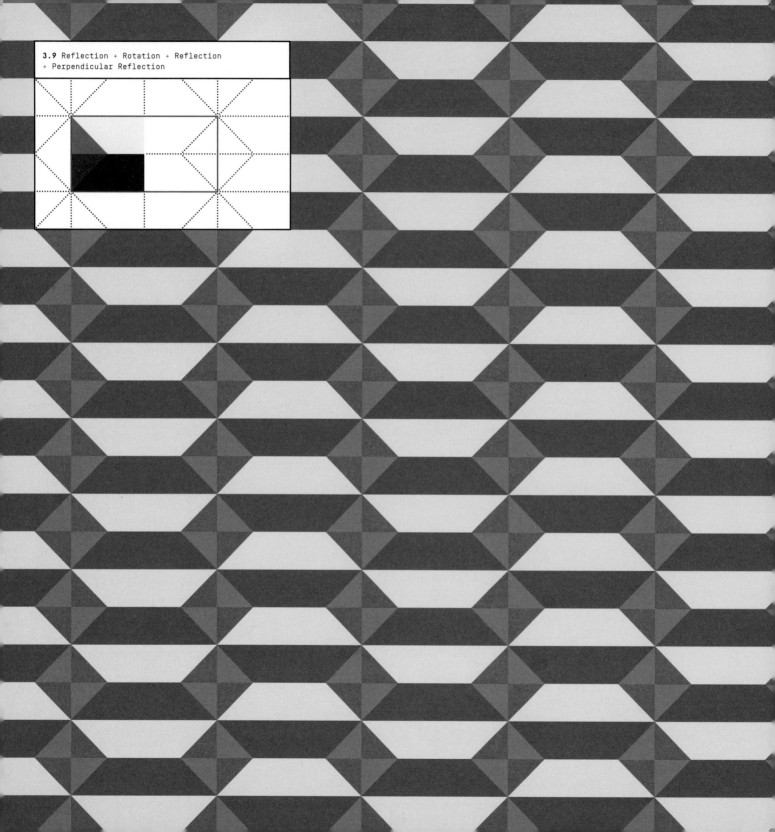

3.9 Reflection + Rotation + Reflection
+ Perpendicular Reflection

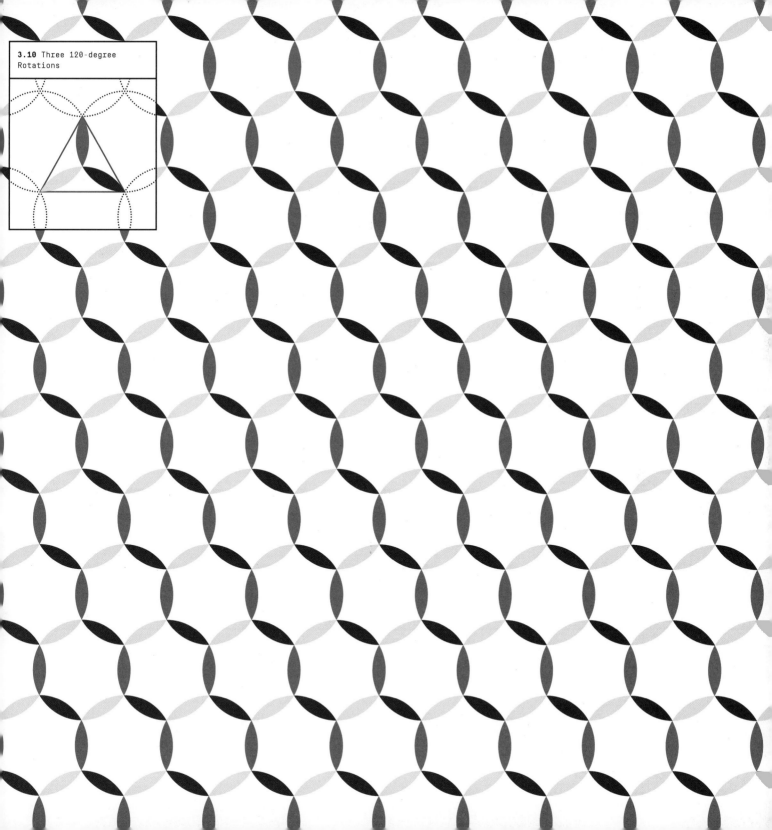

3.10 Three 120-degree
Rotations

3.11 Reflections in an Equilateral Triangle

This second example of creating repeat patterns on a 60-degree triangular grid features an order 3 rotation around a point, in which each element is the reflection of its neighbours across the three sides of each cell. The result is a repeat pattern that is both visually dynamic (a characteristic typical of rotation symmetry) and balanced (a characteristic typical of reflection symmetry).

In this basic example, the element, the upper case letterform L, is rotated and reflected through 60 degrees. This double element is then rotated twice through 120 degrees to create a full 360-degree rotation of six elements. Each element is a reflection of its neighbours.

When developing a repeat pattern using this symmetry operation, it is easier to regard each individual element as a cell. The six cells together will create a hexagon, which will tile with other hexagons to create a grid of equilateral triangles. Note how each corner of each six-cell hexagon becomes a point of rotation. The full repeat pattern has three different points of rotation. Study the repeat pattern with care; it is surprisingly complex.

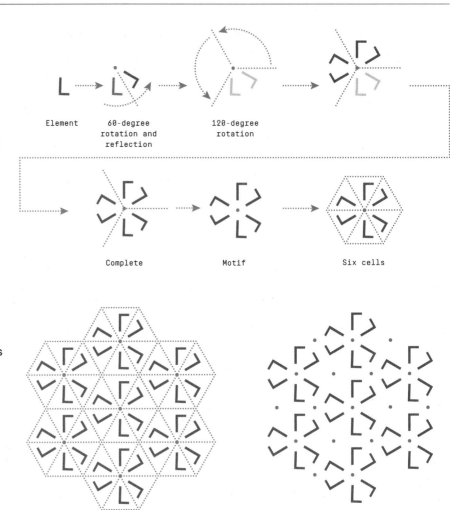

Element   60-degree rotation and reflection   120-degree rotation

Complete   Motif   Six cells

Cell + motif   Complete

Orientation of the Element

By placing the element and the point of
rotation in different orientations to each
other, different repeat patterns can develop.
In this example, a clear pattern of triangles
and hexagons emerges, in contrast to the
pattern seen in the basic example on the
opposite page. It is very difficult to predict
which pattern will emerge from which
orientation of the element, so experiment
as much as possible.

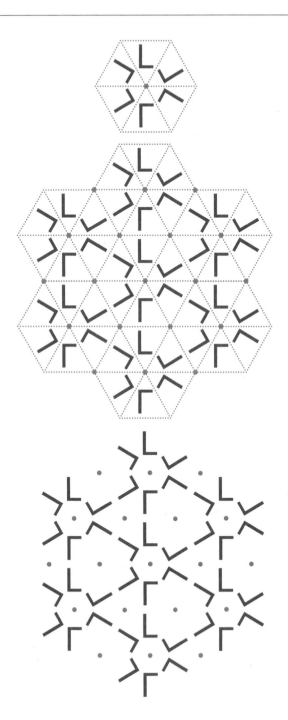

3.12 Reflections of 120-degree Rotations

Although denser and more versatile than the triangular grids introduced previously, the sequence of rotations and reflections that creates this repeat grid is pleasingly simple. A comparison with the previous example is particularly useful.

In this basic example, the element, the lower case letterform f, is turned twice through 120 degrees around a point of rotation to create an order 3 rotation. The motif of three elements makes the cell. The cell is reflected, then turned twice through 120 degrees around a point of rotation to create a hexagon of six cells of order 3 rotation. The cell can be rotated to another orientation around the motif, thus changing the characteristics of the repeat pattern.

To create a repeat pattern, the hexagons are tiled. Note how in this example the edge of each triangular cell is fronted by two elements that are reflected across the edge. In other examples, there might only be one element.

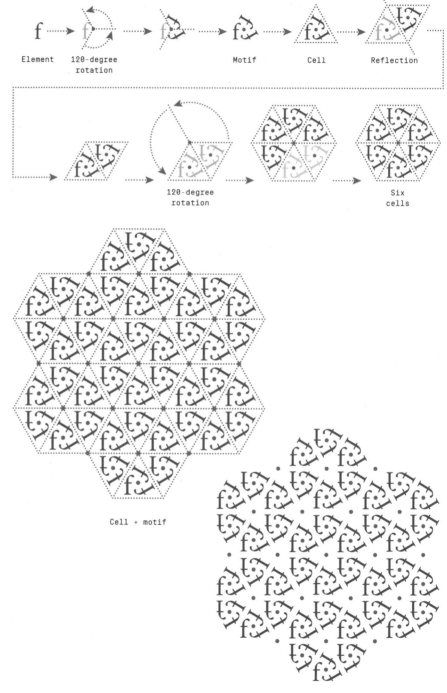

Orientation of the Element

The 18 elements spread around six cells
enable many repeat patterns to be made. The
key is the initial orientation of the element to
the point of rotation in the middle of each cell.
The orientation of the triangular cell around
the three elements is also important.

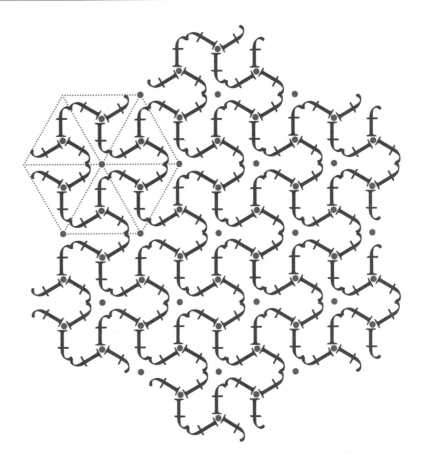

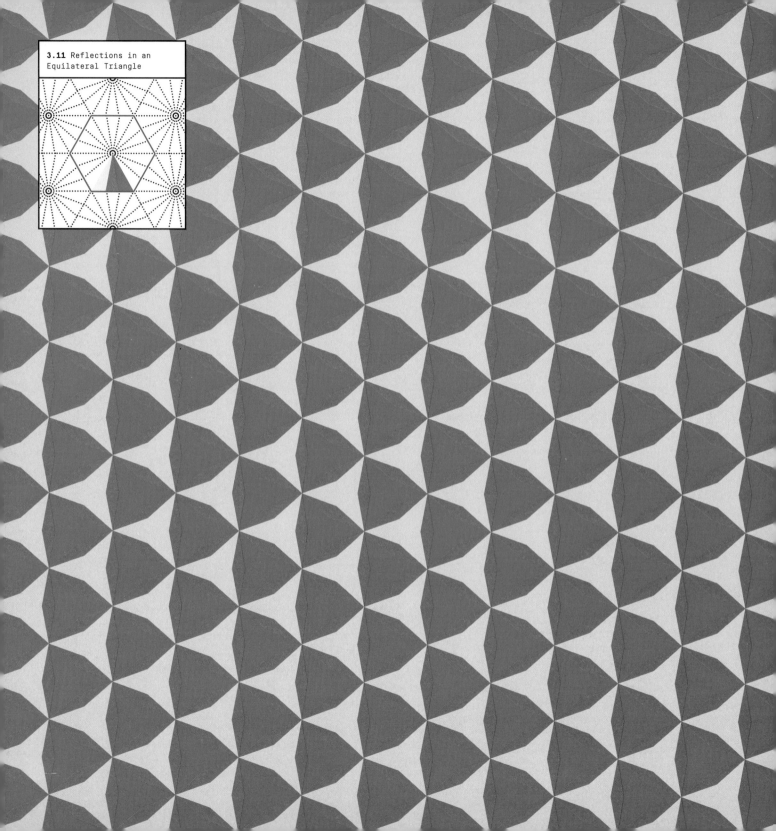

3.11 Reflections in an
Equilateral Triangle

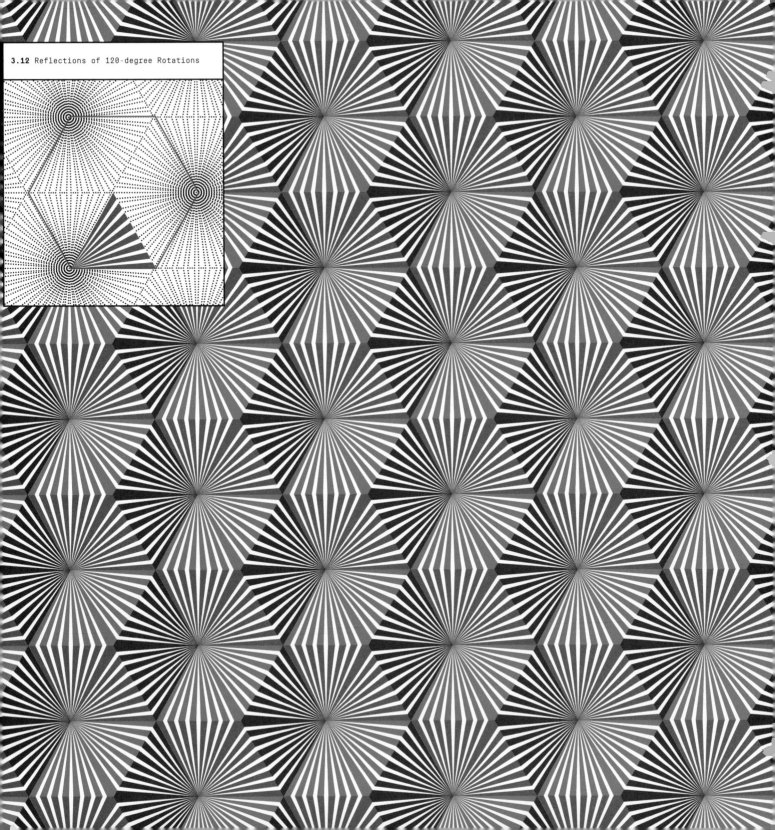

3.12 Reflections of 120-degree Rotations

3.13 90-degree Rotations

This 90-degree geometry planar symmetry is constructed in exactly the same way as the 60- and 120-degree examples on pages 88–91, but achieves a different effect by the use of a different system of tiling: that is, the tiling of 90-degree squares (not 60-degree triangles) to create an order 4 rotation. The result is a very stable rhythmic repeat pattern.

In this basic example, the element, the upper case letterform P, is turned around a point of rotation, each time moving through 90 degrees. The motif thus consists of four elements. The point of rotation is in the middle of the cell, and it can be orientated at any angle around the motif.

To create a repeat pattern, the square cell is tiled across the plane. Note how in this example the corners of each cell also become centres of rotation, but of eight elements, not four. The sequence of symmetry operations to create this eight-fold rotation is complex and deserves study. However, in the examples shown on the opposite page, there are only ever four elements, never eight.

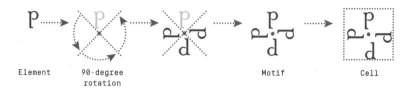

Element   90-degree   Motif   Cell
           rotation

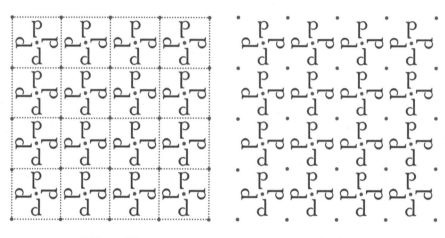

Cell + motif

Complete

Orientation of the Element
The four examples here each place the element in a different orientation from the point of rotation, generating three different repeat patterns. The first example places the point of rotation within the element, thus creating a tight motif and a small cell. The other examples are more open, creating a pleasing relationship between the elements and the spaces around them.

3.14 Reflections of 90-degree Rotations

At first glance, this planar symmetry operation may seem identical to the previous one, but a closer look will reveal the addition here of a reflection symmetry operation between adjacent cells. This second operation adds another level of symmetry to the repeat pattern, complicating the symmetry but, paradoxically, giving greater order to the visual pattern. The same element – a lower case p – is used in both symmetry operations, for ease of comparison between the two.

In this basic example, the element, the lower case letterform p, is turned around a point of rotation, each time moving through 90 degrees to create an order 4 rotation. These four elements are then reflected across a vertical line of symmetry, after which the eight elements are reflected across a horizontal line of symmetry, to create a final motif of sixteen elements. The cell is square.

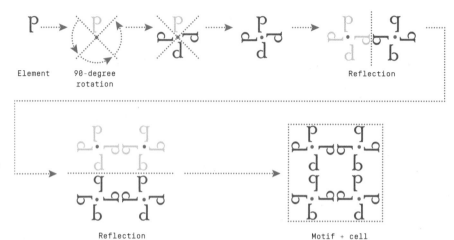

Element   90-degree
          rotation

Reflection

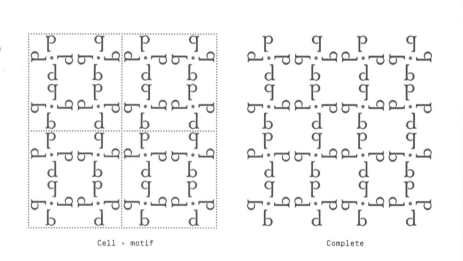

Reflection

Motif + cell

Cell + motif

Complete

Orientation of the Element

As always, placing the element at a different orientation to the point of rotation will create a different repeat pattern. It is worth noting that a cell can be made from any 4 x 4 grid of elements, first nominating any of the sixteen elements to be in a corner of the cell and building the grid from that. However, though there are sixteen elements in any cell, only eight unique cells can be formed. This is because the configuration of elements in one half of a cell repeats that of the other half, and thus unique grids can only be formed by beginning with the elements in one half.

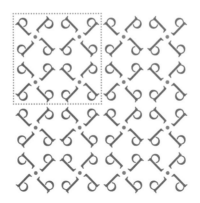

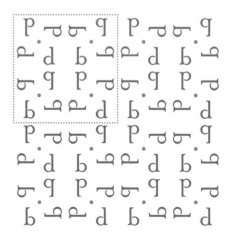

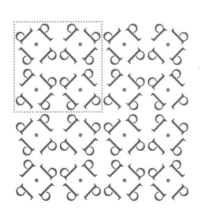

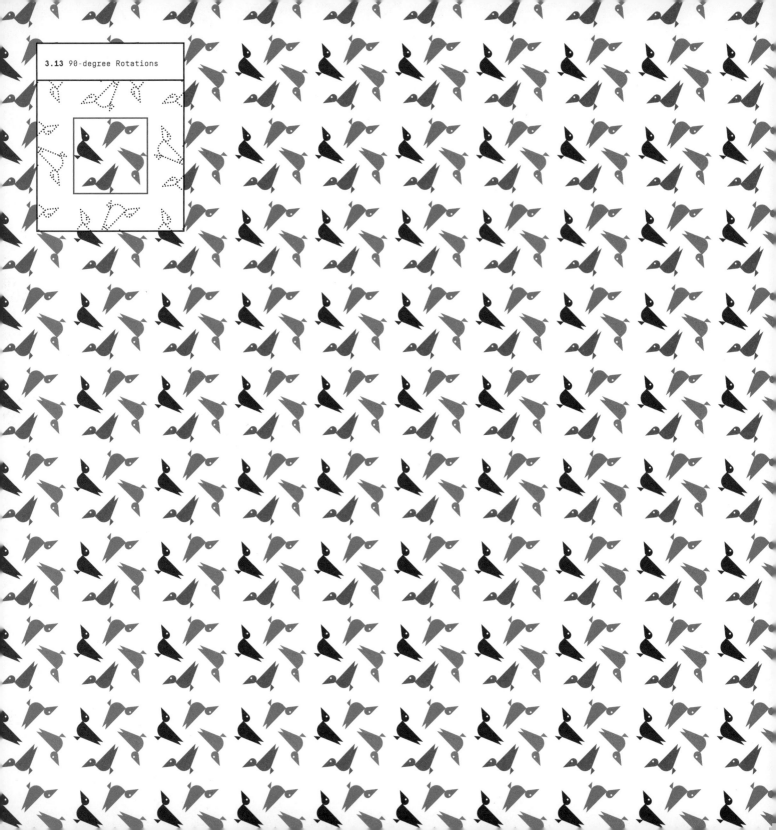

3.13 90-degree Rotations

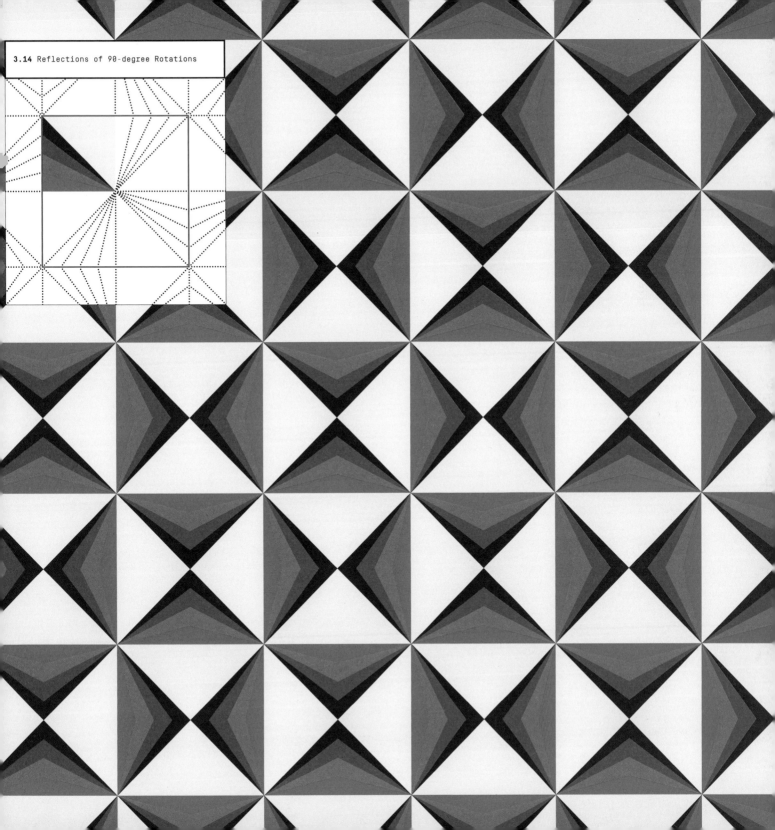

3.14 Reflections of 90-degree Rotations

3.15 Reflections of a 45–45–90-degree Triangle

We have previously seen order 2, order 3, order 4 and order 6 rotations around a point. Now, for the first and only time with planar symmetry, we are dividing the full rotation of 360 degrees into eight parts of 45 degrees each. However, since each part is a reflection of its neighbours to both sides, this is only an order 4 rotation, not order 8. This sequence of reflections and rotations creates a square cell.

In this basic example, the element, the lower case letterform g, is placed inside a triangular cell with angles of 45, 45 and 90 degrees. The element in its cell is reflected across its longest edge to create a second element and a double cell that is square. This square is then rotated four times around a central point (an order 4 rotation) to create a larger square of eight elements and eight triangular cells. The repeat pattern is made from tiling the eight-cell square across the plane.

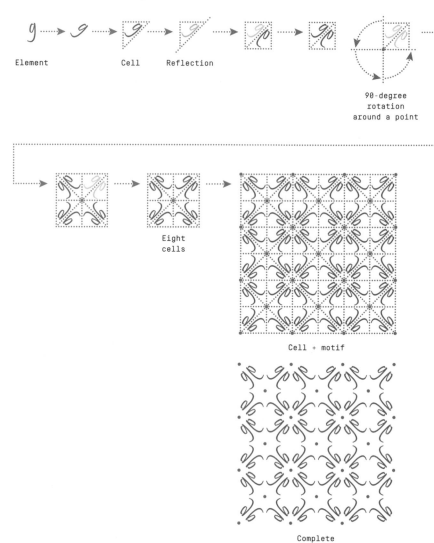

Element   Cell   Reflection

90-degree
rotation
around a point

Eight
cells

Cell + motif

Complete

Orientation of the Element

By placing the element g in different locations within the triangular cell, different repeat patterns can be created. Note that one 45-degree corner of each individual cell will become the centre of the eight cells, and the other 45-degree corner will become half of an eight-cell corner. When a repeat pattern is created, eight of these 45-degree corners will combine to create a second point of rotation where eight 45-degree corners meet. The first example shows how these two possible repeat patterns relate and overlap.

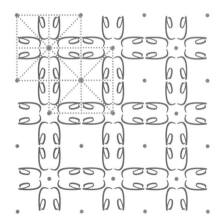
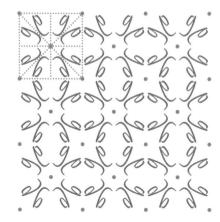

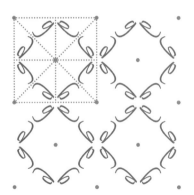
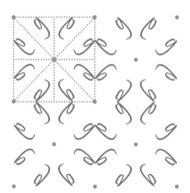

3.16 60-degree Rotations

Here is a pleasingly simple symmetry operation that is easy to explain and understand. It is the order 6 member of the Rotation family that also includes order 3 and order 4 (see page 23). Together, the three operations comprise the full set of regular rotations, and tile the plane with triangles, squares and hexagons.

In this basic example, the element, the lower case letterform p, is turned through 360 degrees in six successive 60-degree rotations to create a motif of six elements. The cell is a regular hexagon. A repeat pattern is created by tiling the hexagons across the plane.

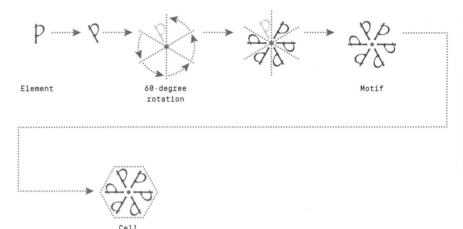

Element   60-degree   Motif
                         rotation

Cell

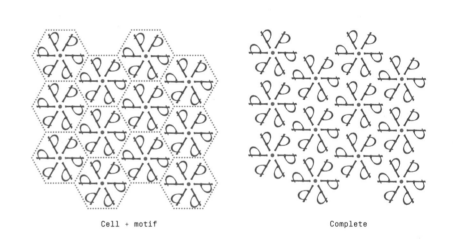

Cell + motif   Complete

Orientation of the Element

The orientation of the element to the point of rotation will determine the characteristics of the repeat pattern. Sometimes the pattern will appear continuous across the plane (as can be seen here in the two examples at the bottom), whereas at other times each cell will appear to be a separate entity (as can be seen in the two examples at the top).

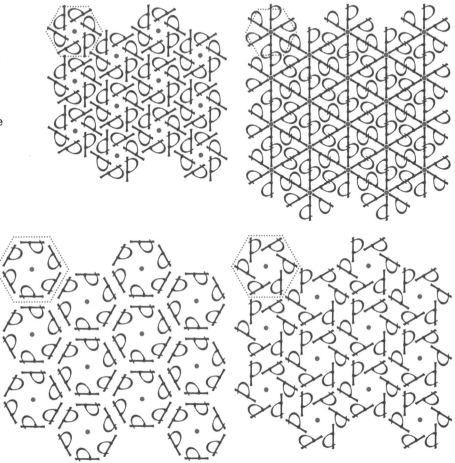

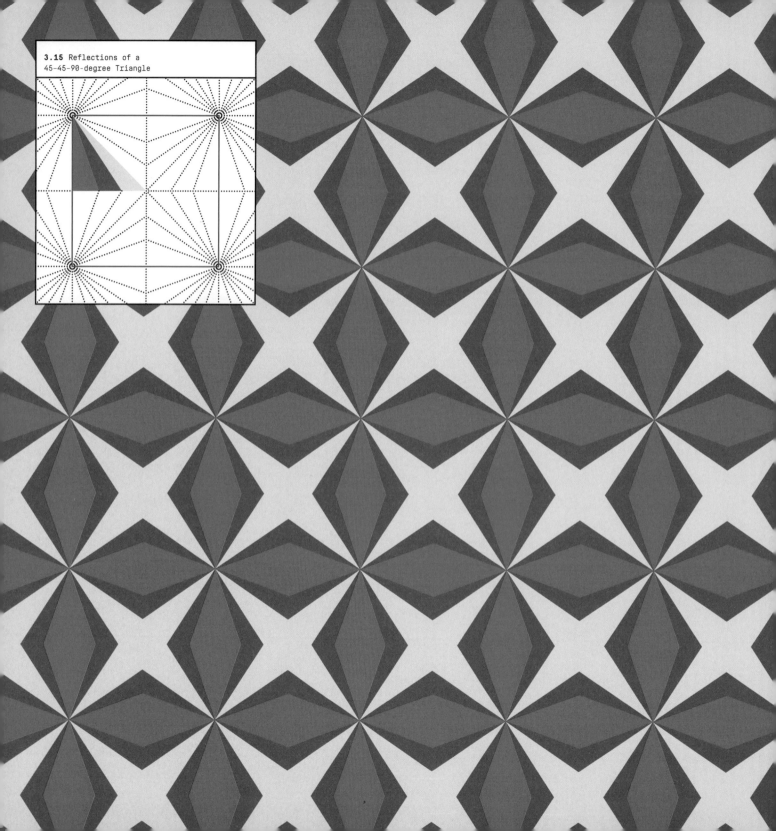

3.15 Reflections of a
45-45-90-degree Triangle

3.16 60-degree Rotations

3.17 Reflections on the Sides of a 30–60–90-degree Triangle

This is the only planar symmetry operation to feature 12 elements, which is achieved by dividing a hexagon into 12 equal triangles. The shape of these triangles is necessarily unusual: they have angles of 30, 60 and 90 degrees. Nevertheless, they tile together well to create equilateral triangles (in which all the angles are 60 degrees) and hexagons.

In this basic example, the element, the lower case letterform j, is placed inside a triangular cell with angles of 30, 60 and 90 degrees. The element is reflected across the side connecting the 30- and 90-degree corners to create an equilateral triangle with two elements. This triangle is then rotated through 360 degrees six times (an order 6 rotation) to create a hexagon of six triangles and twelve elements. A repeat pattern is created simply by tiling the hexagons across the plane. Note how each element reflects across the three sides of the 30–60–90-degree triangle to create a complex web of reflections both inside the cells and across their borders.

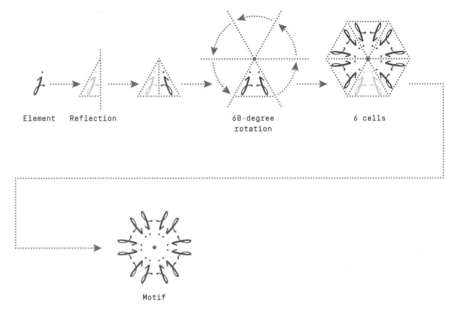

Element   Reflection

60-degree
rotation

6 cells

Motif

Orientation of the Element

The orientation of the element within its cell will determine the characteristics of the repeat pattern. It is interesting to ponder again here what constitutes a cell. Is it the single 30–60–90 triangle with one element, or the 60–60–60 triangle with two elements, or even the hexagon with twelve elements? There is no single answer! However, by considering each of these possibilities in turn, the number and type of symmetry operations, the repeat pattern and also how the elements are coloured (with two, three, four, six or more colours symmetrically arrayed) can be changed. The example at the bottom left shows some of the ways in which single 30–60–90 cells can be combined to create larger cells that will fit together to repeat across the plane. As always, taking as much time as possible to experiment playfully will produce new information about the repeat and so create new patterns.

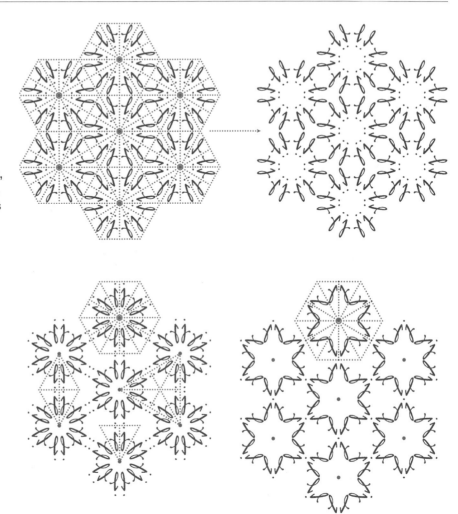

4. Tiling

In their purest form, tiles are identical polygons that repeat across a two-dimensional surface, and that fit together without gaps between them. They are similar to the cells seen frequently in the book to this point, but differ in that whereas a cell defines the perimeter of a combination of symmetry operations, a tile is a simple polygonal element, and could even be blank.

Tiles are limited to quadrilaterals with at least one pair of parallel edges, equilateral and isosceles triangles and hexagons. The rule here is that for tiles to fit together without gaps, the sum of the angles when three or more polygons meet must total exactly 360 degrees (the number of degrees around a point). Despite the relatively small number of eligible polygons, it includes almost all those that are most useful when making repeat patterns, and there is a satisfyingly large number of ways in which they can be placed together across a two-dimensional surface to create repeat patterns.

Semi-regular tiling patterns can be made using more than one type of polygon that fit together without gaps (such as an octagon combined with a square) and non-tessellating tile patterns can be made with polygons such as the seven-sided heptagon, which fit together with gaps in the repeat. Finally, tiling patterns can be made by overlaying two or more grids of lines.

Of all the chapters in the book, this one offers the best opportunities for playful creativity, while still keeping the geometry simple.

4.1 Quadrilateral Tiling

Square Tiles

We used cells throughout Chapter 3. Cells are the polygonal boundaries between the repeats in a repeat pattern and can contain an element, motif or meta-motif. In this chapter, the cells are unassigned, which means they do not contain a graphic image to be repeated. When unassigned, they are tiles. For this reason, they have a black boundary instead of the red boundary associated with cells. Of course, any graphic image can be assigned to a tile – it could be black and white, colourful, a photograph, a scan, a floral print … anything!

These cells tend to be arranged across a plane following one of the 17 planar symmetry operations described in Chapter 3, but the arrangement can be much more unorthodox and creative, while still being in repeat.

Element + cell

Motif + cell

Meta-motif
+ cell

Unassigned tile

Grid Repeats

The simplest arrangement of the square tiles is in a grid. Here are just a few examples, but there are many others. Note that sometimes there are spaces between the tiles.

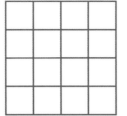
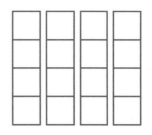
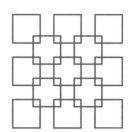
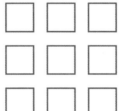
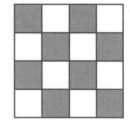

Stepped Repeats

Instead of placing tiles in tidy rows and columns as shown above, they can be stepped to create more complex repeats.

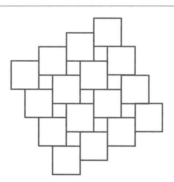
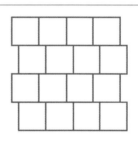
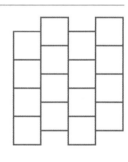

Angled Repeats

There is no reason why the tiles should be arranged along horizontal and vertical lines. They can be rotated to any angle. Usually, these rotations are derived from the grid or stepped repeats above.

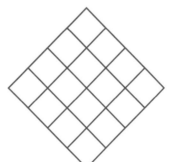
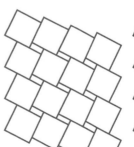
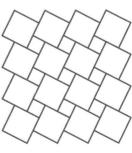

4.1 Quadrilateral Tiling

Rectangular Tiles

Rectangular tiles offer many more possibilities for creating repeat patterns than squares. This is because they have sides of two different lengths, thus allowing two tiles to relate in three possible ways: short to short, long to long and short to long.

Here are a few of the more useful tiling patterns that can be made with rectangles. To create the angled repeats on page 111, simply rotate one of these patterns.

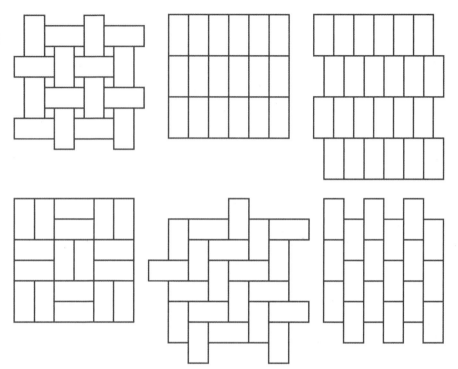

Rhombic and Trapezium Tiles

The inclined sides of rhombic tiles create more dynamic grids than square or rectangular tiles. They are a good alternative for the designer tiring of 90-degree angles and the ubiquitous square grid.

Rhombic tiles can have two pairs of parallel sides (parallelogram and rhombus) or just one pair (trapezium). It is not possible to tile quadrilaterals that have four different angles and four different side lengths without leaving spaces in the repeat.

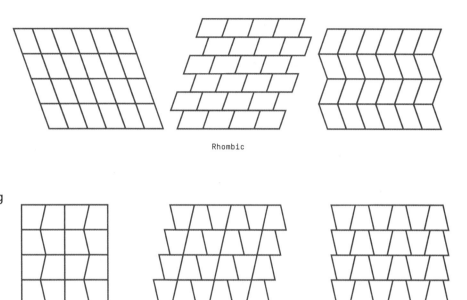

Rhombic

Trapezium

4.2 Triangular Tiling

Triangular tiles offer as many, if not more, possibilities for creating repeat patterns as the more familiar quadrilaterals, with the bonus that the geometry is unusual. Add rotation and reflection to the contents of a cell for even more patterns.

Equilateral Triangles
Equilateral triangles are the simplest triangles to tile because their sides and angles are equal.

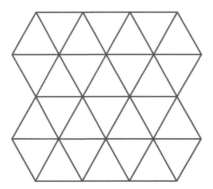 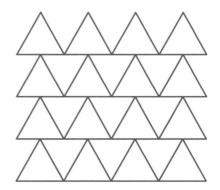

Isosceles Triangles
Equilateral triangles can be stretched or squashed to create triangles that are taller or shorter, wider or narrower. However, if two sides and angles remain equal, as they are in isosceles triangles, it is still simple to tile them in a variety of different ways, a few of which are shown here.

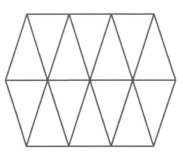 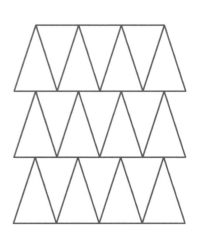

Scalene Triangles

Triangles can also be made to tile if all three sides and angles are different, as they are in scalene triangles. For the tiling to be done without spaces, the triangles must be arranged in rows or columns.

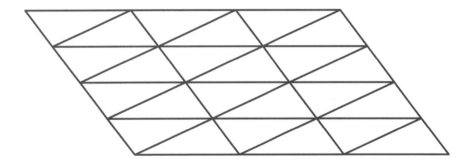

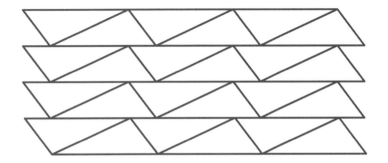

Dividing Squares

There are a great many ways to divide a square into triangles, then tile the repeat across the plane. It is also possible to divide hexagons into triangles and triangles into smaller triangles. Triangular tiles of different shapes can also be created by dividing isosceles or scalene triangles, rectangles and other quadrilaterals, and even octagons and other higher-order polygons.

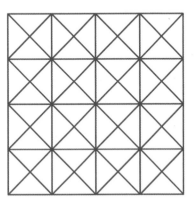

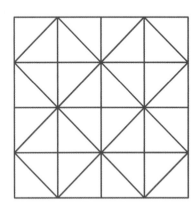

4.1 Quadrilateral Tiling

4.1 Quadrilateral Tiling

4.2 Triangular Tiling

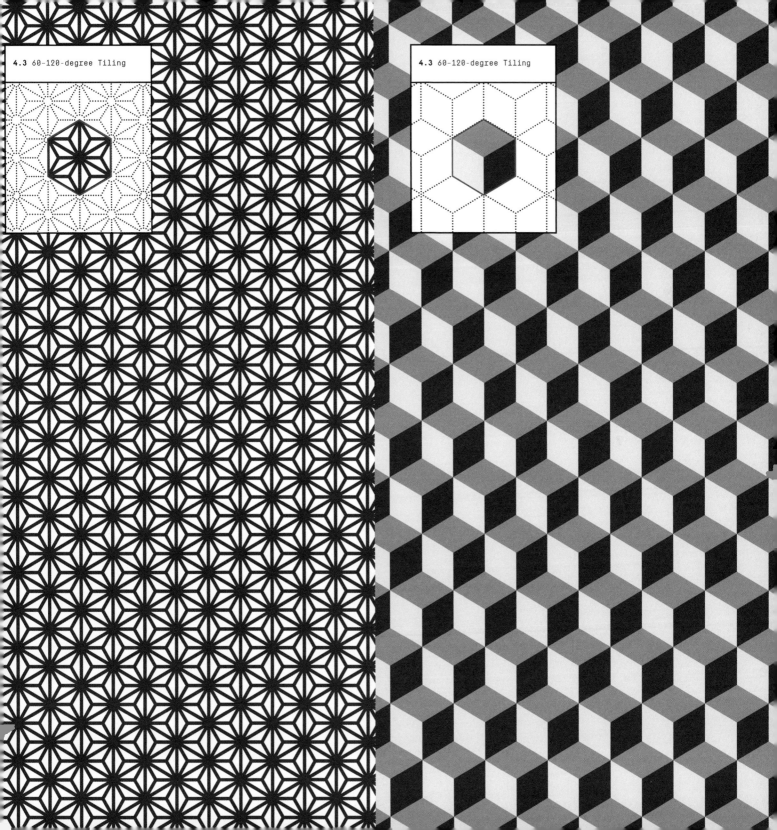

4.3 60-120-degree Tiling

4.3 60-120-degree Tiling

4.3 60–120-degree Tiling

The angles inside a regular hexagon are 120 degrees, double the angle of 60 degrees inside an equilateral triangle. The two polygons, therefore, have a close geometric relationship which can be exploited to create a wide range of tiling patterns that use the two angles.

Hexagons Only

Hexagons can be tiled across a plane without spaces but, more interestingly, they can also touch corner to corner, edge to edge or overlap in a variety of interesting ways, to create 120–60-degree rhombuses of different sizes. Here are a few examples. The first example (top left) is easy to read as a series of hexagons, but some of the others will take a little time to deconstruct.

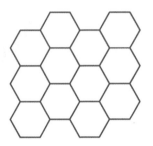
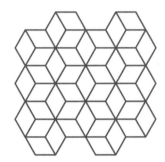
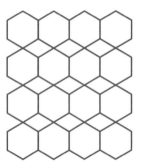
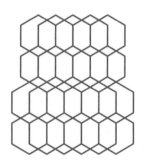

Equilateral Triangles Only

Similarly, equilateral triangles can be arranged in a number of configurations to create tiles that are triangular, rhombic or hexagonal, sometimes mixing them together on the plane in different combinations. As with the previous example, it can take a little time to deconstruct the patterns and find the equilateral triangles of equal size.

Other Triangular Tiles
Equilateral triangles can be divided into
smaller triangles that will tile without spaces.

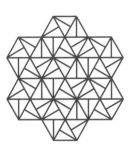

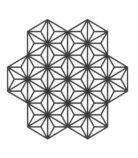

Rotational Tiling
An interesting variation is to use rotation
symmetry (see page 22) to create a tiling
pattern around a central point, then to repeat
the pattern at ever-smaller or ever-larger
scales around the same point. This tiles a
plane not by repeating identical tiles across
the surface, but by increasing the scale of the
tile. It is an example of fractal mathematics,
in which a pattern recurs at different scales.

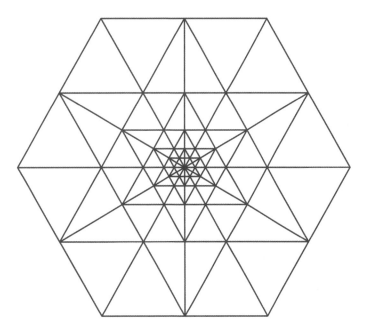

4.4 Semi-regular Tiling

Semi-regular means that a plane is tiled with tiles of more than one shape, each of which is a regular polygon. By expanding the rule of tiling with only one polygon, many more interesting possibilities appear. However, semi-regular tiling still has its own rules, most notably that the polygons are regular, meaning that only equilateral triangles, squares, hexagons, octagons and dodecagons (12-sided polygons) may be used, as these are the only polygons that will tile in a repeat pattern without creating irregular spaces between the tiles. This means, rather fascinatingly, that all the edges in the tile pattern will be the same length.

Motifs that are entirely different in colour and texture can be used in each of the two polygons, thus creating a double pattern. Alternatively, one of the polygons can be left as a void. Tiles can be rotated and/or reflected, following the principles discussed in Chapter 3.

Two Polygonal Tiles
In these examples, two different regular polygons are used to tile the plane without spaces. The most commonly used polygon is the equilateral triangle, whose small 60-degree corner means that it can tile with a wider variety of options than polygons with larger corner angles.

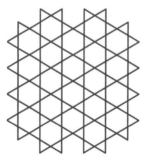

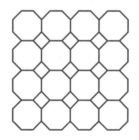

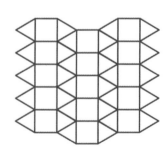

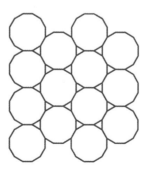

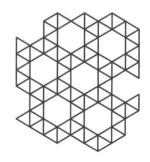

Three Polygonal Tiles

In a few cases, as many as three regular polygons can be used to tile a surface. Three different motifs can be created, one for each type of polygon, or one of the polygons can be left as a void. The possibilities for creating rich and complex patterns are endless.

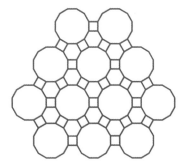
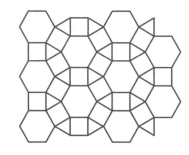

Other Polygonal Tiles

There are are great many polygons that tile well. One example is given here. The basic pentagonal tile is not a regular pentagon – rotating from the top, it has angles of 135, 90, 112.5, 112.5 and 90 degrees. The effect is to create the illusion of a grid of overlapping hexagons, similar to the grids discussed on page 118.

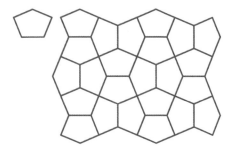
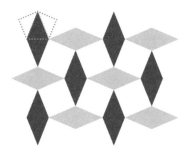

The pentagons can be subdivided into three triangles. Two of the triangles have angles of 45–45–90 degrees and one has angles of 67.5–67.5–45 degrees. These triangles can be combined together in many different configurations to create a series of larger triangles, squares, rhombuses, trapeziums, deltoids and other polygons, thus forming a great many unusual tiling patterns, a few examples of which are shown here.

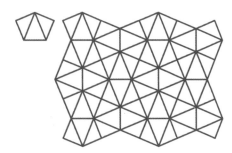

4.5 Non-tessellating Tiling

It is possible to tile polygons either edge to
edge or corner to corner, leaving irregular
spaces between them. These non-
tessellating tile patterns create a complexity
of relationships that is difficult to create with
regular tiling patterns, thus creating a rich
alternative aesthetic. As with regular tiling
patterns, only some polygons will fit with
others, so the possibilities are not infinite.
A few examples are given here, but there
are many others to find. The repeat patterns
shown here all feature polygons touching
edge to edge or corner to corner. There
is a further, much larger, set of polygons
that touch corner to edge, or float in space
without touching.

Pentagon Tiles
Multiples of the 108-degree interior angle
of a pentagon will not exactly fill the 360
degrees of a circle, so it is impossible to tile
pentagons on a flat plane without leaving
spaces between them. Nevertheless, it is
possible to arrange pentagons in several
different ways to create repeat patterns of
varying complexity. Note that the example on
the right is an example of order 5 rotation
symmetry (see page 23) that will continue to
expand infinitely outwards.

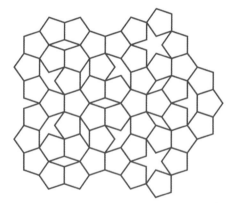
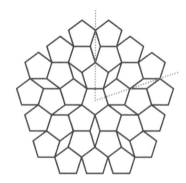

Heptagon Tiles
Of all the basic polygons, heptagons (which
have seven sides) remain largely unused,
unknown and unloved. Their asymmetry and
unwieldy interior angle of 51.428 degrees
win them few friends. Nevertheless, they
can still be tiled, albeit with spaces between
them. If you're looking to find unfamiliar repeat
patterns, exploring the tiling potential of the
heptagon will give you interesting results.

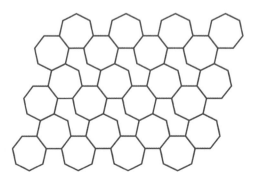

Nonagon and Decagon Tiles

The nonagon (with nine sides) and the decagon (with ten sides) will tile with irregular spaces, but the possibilities are fewer than for a heptagon. Other higher-order polygons with eleven sides, thirteen sides and more will also tile irregularly, but the repeats become increasingly difficult to find and increasingly fewer in number as the number of sides increases.

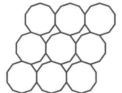

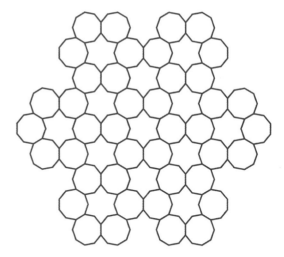

Multiple Polygons

Here, a square and a hexagon tile together, leaving a star-shaped space. An alternative description is to say that a hexagon is tiling with other rotated hexagons to leave spaces that are squares and stars. Can you find other combinations of two or more polygons that will tile to create a repeat pattern, but with spaces?

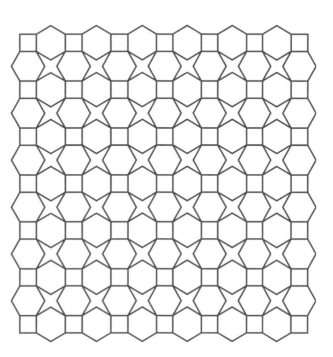

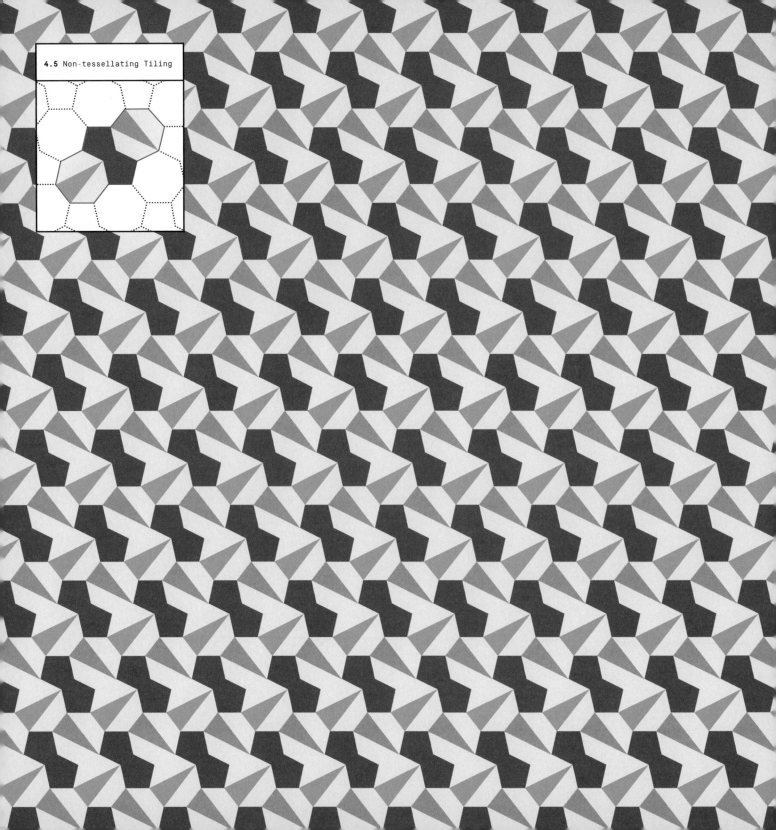

4.5 Non-tessellating Tiling

4.6 Superimposition
of Grid Lines

4.6 Superimposition
of Grid Lines

4.6 Superimposition of Grid Lines

If you look again through this chapter and Chapter 3, you will find that some of the cell or tile patterns made of connected polygons can also be interpreted as a series of long lines – sometimes straight and sometimes zigzag – that snake from one side of the pattern to the other, the crossing points of which become the corners of the polygons. Thus, while cell and tile patterns can be created by aligning polygons, many others can also be created by criss-crossing long lines. This radically different method of constructing repeat patterns can be as simple or as complex as required, and often creates pleasing and unexpected results.

Straight-line Grids

An endless series of square, rectangular and rhombic grids can be created by overlaying lines at 90 degrees or at another angle. Sometimes all the tiles will be identical, and sometimes there will be two, three or more different tiles that tessellate, depending on the complexity of the lines.

The final example shows three lines overlaid at an angle of 120 degrees to each other. The result is a grid of equilateral triangles. By overlaying the three grids differently, or by using different spacing between the lines, more complex grids of triangles and other polygons can be created.

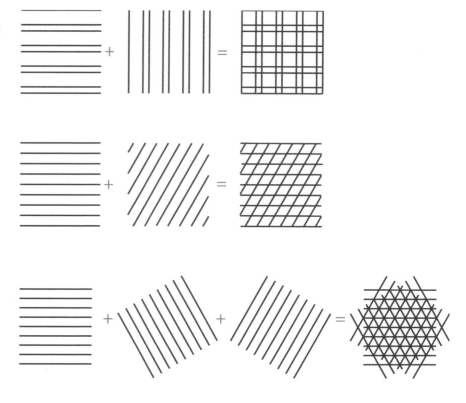

Stepped-line Grids

Grids of stepped or zigzag lines can
be overlaid to create tiles of surprising
complexity. The two lines can be the same
or different. It is also possible, as in the final
example, to create a line, reflect it, then
repeat this double-line motif across the plane.
Look carefully at the six examples here. They
all use zigzag lines in a different way.

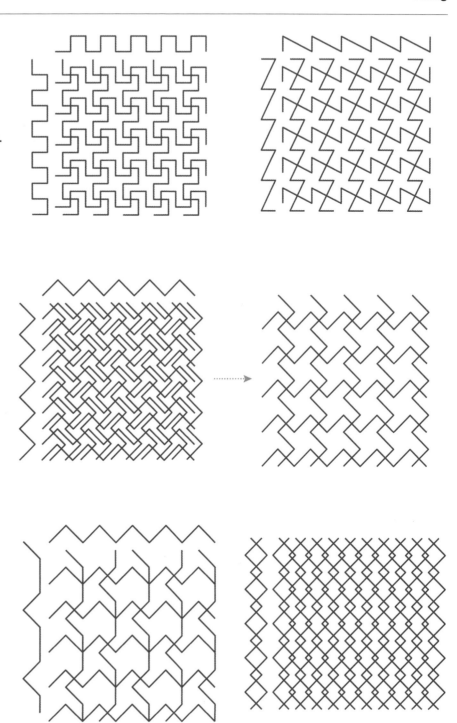

5. Seamless & Escher-type Repeats

We have all seen the mesmerizing effect in bolts of fabric in which a complex pattern repeats itself endlessly, without an apparent beginning or end and without any obvious boundary between the repeats. The effect of a seamless repeat, sometimes known a wallpaper repeat, can seem magical and difficult to achieve. However, the method is as simple as it is elegant. With a little practice, it can be used to create repeat patterns that can seem deceptively non-geometric and non-repeat. This book offers simple but powerful methods for making these repeats.

The Dutch graphic artist M.C. Escher (1898–1972) was renowned for creating meticulously realized animals, birds and people that would interlock together without spaces and repeat across a surface. They were created using tiling techniques that almost defy comprehension. While there is no doubting the brilliance of his designs, the method by which they were achieved is surprisingly accessible and is explained here in its square, rectangular, triangular and hexagonal variants.

Although unrelated, the wallpaper and Escher techniques are grouped together in this chapter because they show the extent to which basic tiling patterns can be stretched and squeezed to create patterns far removed from the basic symmetry operations that began the book.

5.1 Seamless Repeats

Basic Method

The method described here is simple and elegant and, once mastered, you will want to use it again and again. The same method should be followed whether you are working digitally or by hand, using scissors, glue and a photocopying machine.

If working digitally, there are many online sites that will make so-called seamless repeats or wallpaper repeats if you input an image. However, most of these have only limited capabilities and are little more than toys. The method described here is more powerful and infinitely versatile.

The realignment of corners ABCD – the heart of the Seamless Repeat method – can be performed using the basic copy and paste commands available with any vector graphic software, or if you use Adobe Photoshop, the offset command will automatically perform this realignment for you. There are many online tutorials.

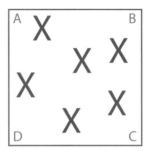

(1) Here is a simple graphic image: six Xs on a square tile. Note that the graphics are kept away from the corners of the tile. This is entirely deliberate and is an important feature of the design. Note also the corners marked A, B, C and D. For clarity, the image here is simple, but your image can be complex, multicoloured, textured, photographic, a print … anything you want. To reiterate: when creating an image on a tile, avoid the corners.

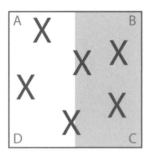

(2) The right-hand half of the tile is here identified by the peach tone. In the next step, we will move it. Note that the letters B and C appear in this half of the tile.

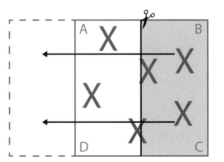

(3) Separate the right-hand half of the tile from the left-hand half and move it across to the left, so that B is next to A and C is next to D. This must be a very accurate cut, exactly down the middle of the tile.

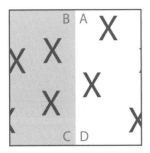

(4) This is the result. Note the new alignment of B with A and C with D.

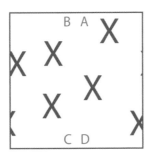

(5) This is the new-look tile. The second stage is to repeat the previous steps, but this time cutting horizontally across the middle.

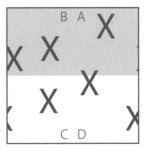

(6) The top half of the tile is here identified by the peach tone. In the next step, we will move it. Note that the letters B and A appear in this half of the tile.

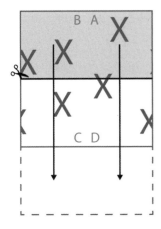

(7) Separate the top half of the tile from the bottom half and move it downwards, so that B and A lie beneath C and D. This must be a very accurate cut, exactly across the middle of the tile.

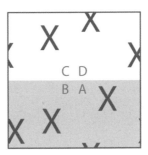

(8) This is the result. Note the grouping of corners CD and BA in the middle of the tile. Note also how one X has separated into two pieces that touch the top and bottom edges of the tile. The separation into two (or even four) pieces of any graphic element is normal and should not be avoided. It is what makes this type of pattern appear seamless.

(9) This is the final tile. If you are using scissors and paper, this tile must now be copied as many times as required to make a repeat pattern. If you are working digitally, remove the black frame and the ABCD.

5.1 Seamless Repeats

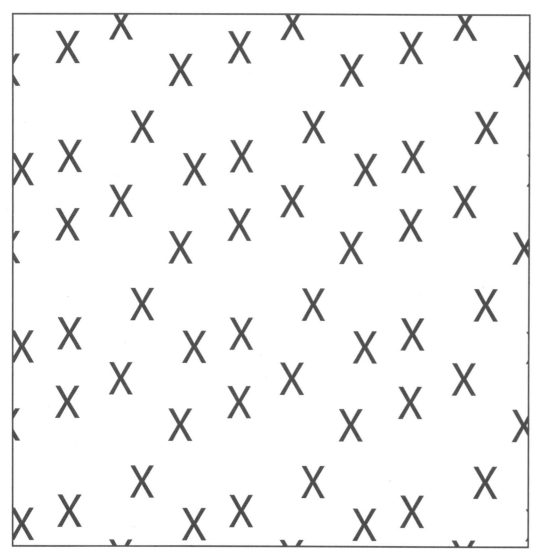

(10) Here is a 3 x 3 grid of the tile seen in the previous step. Note how the Xs that were cut into two pieces have magically reformed so that the boundaries of the repeat are very difficult to see. The result is a pleasing unstructured repeat pattern that may appear random if given just a cursory glance. The tile may also be rectangular instead of square.

The pattern on the facing page, made using this Basic Method, does not appear seamless. However, more elements can be added by following the additional steps described in the Advanced Method on pages 134–136, creating the more seamless pattern on page 137.

Also keep in mind that the tile can be rectangular instead of square.

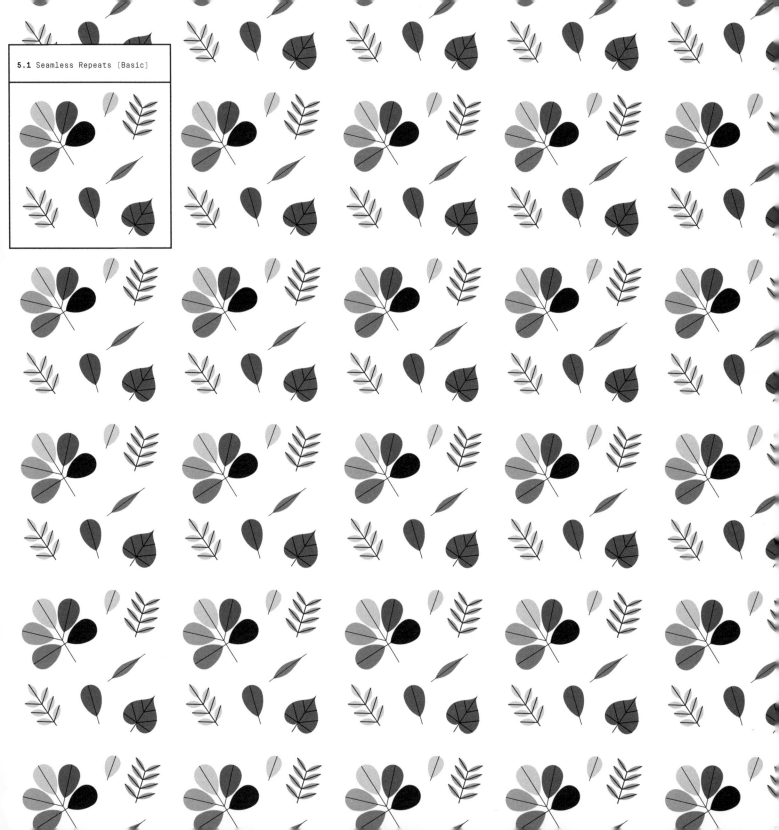

5.1 Seamless Repeats [Basic]

5.1 Seamless Repeats

Advanced Method

When following the basic method on pages 130–132, it is very difficult to predict how the corners of the tile will separate and realign, and thus to predict how the final repeat pattern will look. It is therefore normal practice now to add a second, even a third and fourth layer of graphics to balance the pattern, to fill in any empty spaces and to bring it to a general level of completeness.

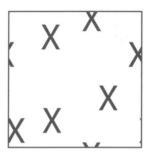

(1) This is the completed tile from the basic method. Note that the centre is empty. This is because you were instructed not to put graphics into the corners. After realignment, those corners become the middle of the tile.

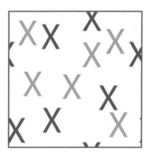

(2) The first task is to fill in the empty centre and some other empty spaces with extra graphics. This could be several small elements (as shown here) or be a continuation of the existing image. For clarity, the new graphic elements are shown in grey. As before, do not place any image into the corners.

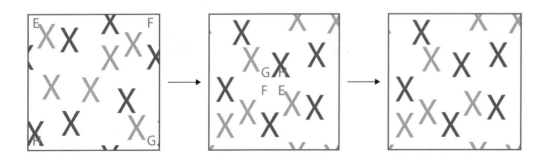

(3) Begin by labelling the corners E, F, G and H. Follow the steps of the basic method until the letters are grouped in the middle. Note that in this realignment, no Xs crossed the horizontal or vertical centre lines of the tile, so no X was separated into pieces and scattered around the sides of the tile. Note also that the new grey Xs have been realigned, and the configuration of blue Xs has reverted back to the original positions that they occupied in the first step of the basic method.

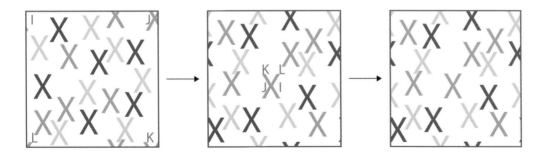

(4) The tile created at the end of the previous step is still a little empty, so some of the spaces can be filled with a new layer of graphics. The new Xs added here are peach. The corners are labelled I, J, K and L and the realignment described in the basic method is performed on the tile for the third time, so that, as before, the letters end up grouped in the middle of the tile. Note how one of the blue Xs in the middle of the tile at the beginning of this step is separated into four pieces by the end of the step.

(5) The tile at the end of the previous step has space in the middle for a fourth layer of graphics, this time Xs in brown. There is no need to perform again the realignment of the corners described in the basic method, because the graphic image and the tile are now complete.

For the purposes of demonstrating the method, four layers of graphics were added and the realignment was performed three times. However, when you create your own tiles, how many times you do it is entirely at your discretion, depending on the complexity of the pattern and personal choice.

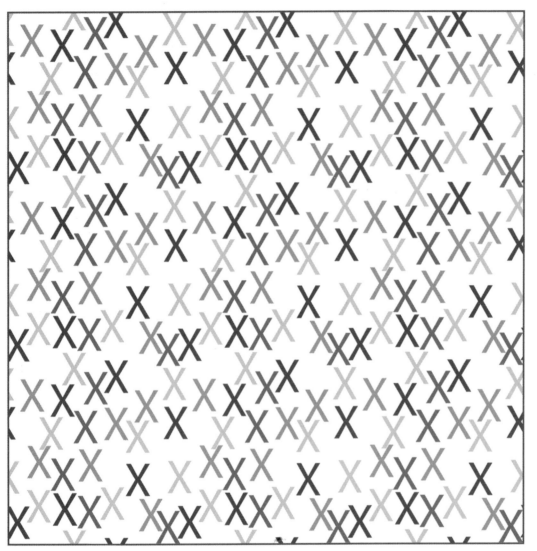

(6) Here is a 3 x 3 grid of the tile in the previous step. Of course, more graphic elements could be added, separated or overlapped, repeating the alignment process described in the basic method as many times as required. There is really no limit. For some people, understanding how this powerful method of generating repeat patterns can be used, extended and pushed to its limits becomes the basis of a career as a surface designer.

The pattern on the facing page is the Basic Method pattern seen on page 133 but with additional elements added as described in the Advanced Method. The result is a complex seamless repeat in which the repeat is difficult to perceive.

It is interesting to compare this seamless repeat with the pattern on the left. All the Xs in the patterns to the left have equal weight, whereas in the pattern to the right, the large, five-leaf element is somewhat dominant in the pattern. This means that the eye picks out the grid of five-leaf elements, and will thus see a repeat pattern. However, the equal weight of all the Xs means that it is more difficult for the eye to perceive a repeat pattern.

So, to create a repeat pattern in which the repeat is very difficult to see, create a repeat that has a large number of small elements of a similar weight and shape, equally spaced.

5.1 Seamless Repeats [Advanced]

5.2 Escher-type Repeats

The remarkable surface patterns of interlocking tiles for which M.C. Escher became renowned were memorable because they were instantly recognizable as detailed animals, birds and figures, rather than as geometric repeats, which is actually what they were underneath. His interlocking repeats were not merely squares and triangles, but simple geometric forms subtly changed to become limbs, heads and wings, made more recognizable by adding detailed graphics that depicted feathers, scales or facial features. The pages that follow describe how to make these interlocking geometric repeats. On pages 142–143, the technique for creating a representational interlocking pattern most associated with M.C. Escher is described. This prepares the method for making the triangular and hexagonal tiles described in the remainder of the chapter by showing how the method of construction works for simpler geometric tiles.

Tiles with Four Unrelated Sides

This is the simplest of the Escher-type repeats and is remarkably versatile. Doodling almost any tile often results in an animal or human form becoming apparent within it.

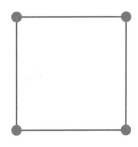

(1) Draw four dots that define the corners of a square. This is the tile. The dots can be connected to create a square, though this is not essential.

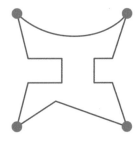

(2) On each of the four sides of the square, doodle simple lines. Be careful not to make the corners too tight or bring the lines too close together.

(3) The square of dots can be extended across the plane to make a repeat pattern. A small 2 x 2 grid like this will tell you if the repeat looks good, or if any of the lines need adjusting to improve the pattern. Note that when all four sides of the square are drawn differently, three different areas will combine to create the repeat.

(4) This is the completed repeat pattern. For clarity, it is rendered with two colours, but it could have been rendered with many. Later in the chapter, we will see how triangles and hexagons can be made to achieve the same effect.

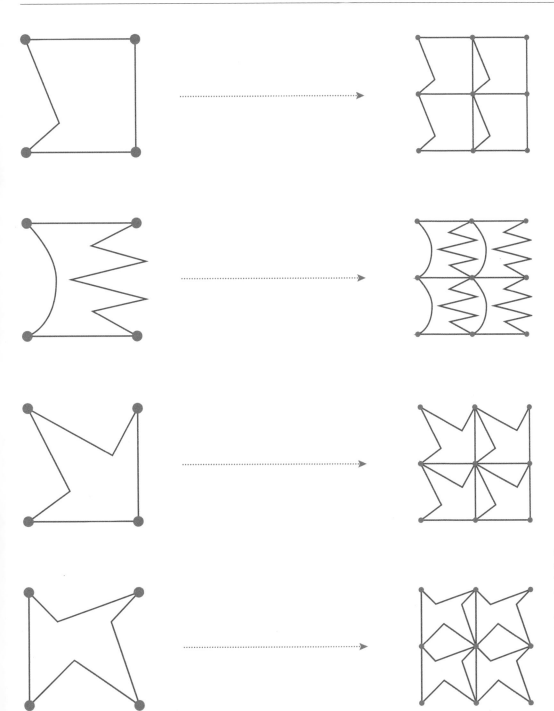

(5) Instead of deforming all four sides of the square, it is possible to deform just one, two or three sides. The patterns will necessarily be simpler than if all four sides are deformed, but many interesting effects can nevertheless be created. Some care needs to be taken not to create awkward spaces between the tiles. These spaces are not just gaps, but are as integral to the overall success of the repeat pattern as the tile itself.

5.2 Escher-type Repeats

Tiles with Identical Opposite Sides

This is the technique most associated with M.C. Escher, because only one tile shape is created, not several, as in the previous examples. If you wish to create an animal or human repeat, design a tile almost at random, then look at it, turning it through 360 degrees to see it from all angles. With some imagination, you will be able to see, for example, a roughly drawn bird or a person running. Then you can begin to change the lines subtly to make the subject more recognizable.

In the example on this page, the final tile looks a little elephant-like. Turned clockwise through 90 degrees, it looks a little rabbit-like. With a little extra work, tiles could be created that were recognizably either subject or perhaps both. This transformation from the abstract to the representational is exacting and is described in detail in the next section.

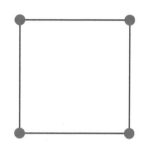

(1) Create a square tile defined by four dots.

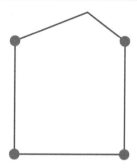

(2) It can be as simple or as complex as you wish.

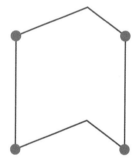

(3) Deform the opposite side in exactly the same way. The two lines must be identical, not reflections.

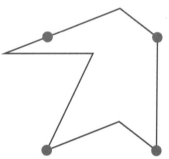

(4) Now deform one of the remaining lines. In this example, the deformation continues the top side in a straight line.

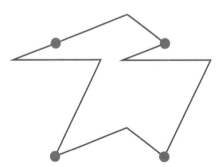

(5) Deform the fourth side as a copy of the third side. The two sides must be identical. If some of the corners look too tight or if lines are too close together, you can change them. Remember: the opposite sides must always be identical, so if you change one side, you must also change the opposite side.

(6) When the single tile has been designed, tile it to create a simple square grid across the plane. The effect of tiling such complex polygons without leaving any spaces is impressive and also enjoyably simple to create.

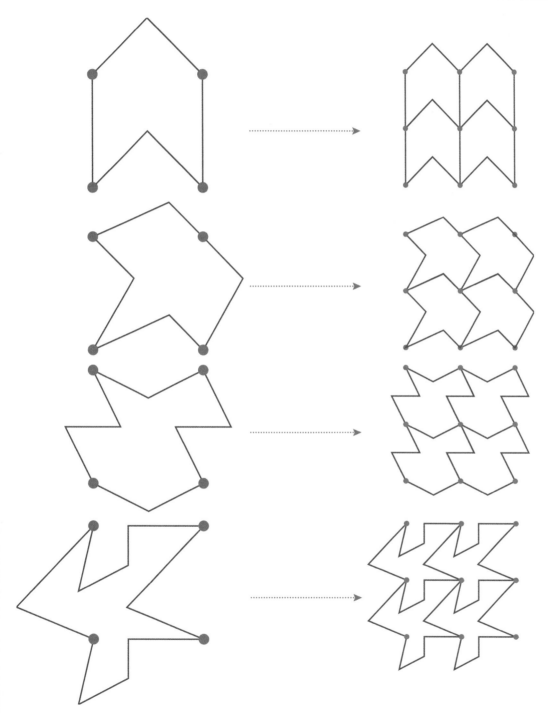

(7) The square tile can be deformed in many ways. The examples here show how tiles can be given any number of edges. Here, they have 6, 7, 10 and 12 edges. Create a simple 2 x 2 grid to see how the tiles look when gridded, make any necessary changes, then create another 2 x 2 grid. Repeat the process as many times as required until you have designed the perfect tile.

Rectangular Tiles

This method is the same as the previous one, except that for variety, the tile is a rectangle, not a square. The difference is that it explains, step by step, how a geometric tile can be transformed into an Escher-like tile of a recognizable subject by carefully adjusting the outline of the tile until the subject becomes clear. This transformational sequence of steps will offer insights into how Escher-type tiles can be created, starting from an unpromising-looking geometric doodle.

(1) This is the basic rectangular tile.

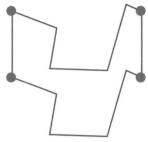

(2) Deform one pair of opposite sides. Here, the top edge of the rectangle is deformed downwards, so the bottom edge must also deform downwards to exactly mimic the path of the top edge. It is generally more useful to deform the sides dramatically, rather than minimally, as this will create a tile that has a more distinctive shape and can therefore be more easily imagined as parts of a recognizable subject such as an animal.

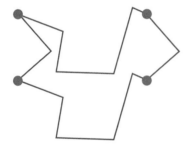

(3) Deform the remaining pair of lines. Be careful to pay some attention to the positions of the already deformed sides, so that the new deformations work comfortably with them. At this stage, the tile happens to look a little like a bird, or perhaps a mammal.

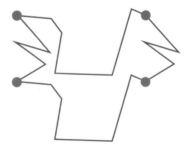

(4) Further deforming the 'head' creates a mouth. The 'tail' end must be identically deformed, which now begins to look a little feathery. Perhaps the tile will be a bird – perhaps a chicken?

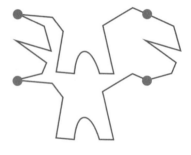

(5) The chicken needs legs. Adding a simple curve to the side at the bottom of the tile creates fore and hind legs, suggesting a mammal rather than a bird. Curved lines are, of course, just as useful as straight lines when outlining abstract or recognizable tiles and should be used whenever appropriate. This curve must be repeated on the top side and begins to look like a wing. Further shaping is given to the head and tail. The tile begins to resemble a fantasy creature: part dragon, part dinosaur.

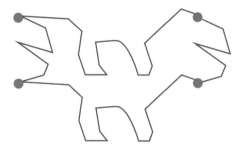

(6) Once the theme is decided, all sides of the tile can be changed to make the subject more recognizable. Here, almost every line has been subtly moved, and the tile has been stretched horizontally, making the body bigger relative to the head and tail. The key element in the success of a design is to ensure that what works for (say) the mouth will work equally well for the tail, because these two lines must be identical. Every line and every corner has its twin at the opposite side of the tile, and all aspects of the silhouette must be respected equally. Adding a solid colour and some carefully chosen graphic lines make the tile recognizable as a baby dragon.

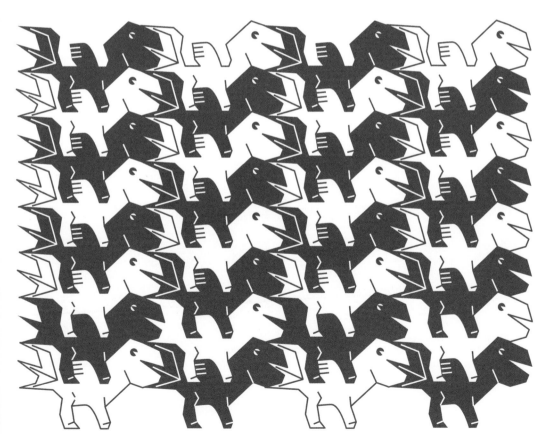

(7) When seen by itself, a single tile looks so complex that it does not seem as though it will repeat … but it does, as is evident in this final grid of rectangular tiles. Although it is a sophisticated repeat pattern, the example given here is relatively simple. M.C. Escher was able to develop the technique much further. For example, he designed tiles that repeated the same subject but facing in different directions (instead of all facing the same way); designed tiles that were all different; designed rotational repeats in which the repeats rotated around a centre point and then either grew in size or diminished as they moved away from it; and designed tiles that slowly metamorphosed from one subject into another. He also used tiles that were triangular or hexagonal, not rectangular, as here. These systems will be explained on the following pages.

5.2 Escher-type Repeats

Triangular Tiles and Rotational Tiling

There are two ways to deform triangular tiles. The first way is to deform two of the three sides of a triangle, then rotate them around a point.

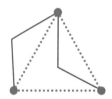

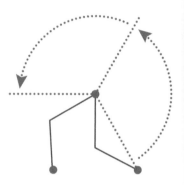

(1) Create an equilateral triangle defined by three dots.

(2) Deform one side of the triangle. Repeat the same deformation with another side, so that the two deformations meet at one corner, here at the top of the triangle. Note that one deformed side will be inside the triangle, while the other will be outside.

(3) This pair of deformed sides occupy 120 degrees of a 360-degree circle and can be repeated twice more to occupy the full 360 degrees (this is an order 3 rotation – see page 23).

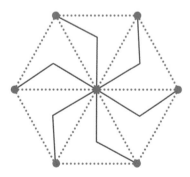

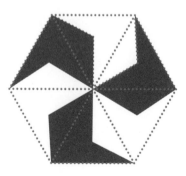

(4) This is the result: a hexagon comprising six equilateral triangles, with six identical radiating lines.

(5) The six identical polygons that meet at the centre of the hexagon can be given alternate colours. Note that the sides of the hexagon are not breached. The breaching of this third side is explained in the next example.

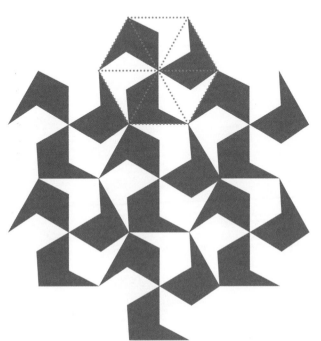

(6) There are two ways to tile identical hexagons. The six sides of the hexagon in the previous step alternate between the two colours. One way to tile the hexagons is to arrange them so that all the blue edges on different tiles touch other blue edges, and the white edges touch other white edges. This is the first example shown here. Note how by connecting blue to blue and white to white, some of the polygons can continue from one hexagon to another to create longer S-shaped polygons.

The second example shown here connects a blue edge of one hexagon with the white edge of another, so that as the hexagons tile across the surface, sides of the same colour never touch. This retains the six comma-shaped polygons within each hexagon and ensures that all the tiles are identical.

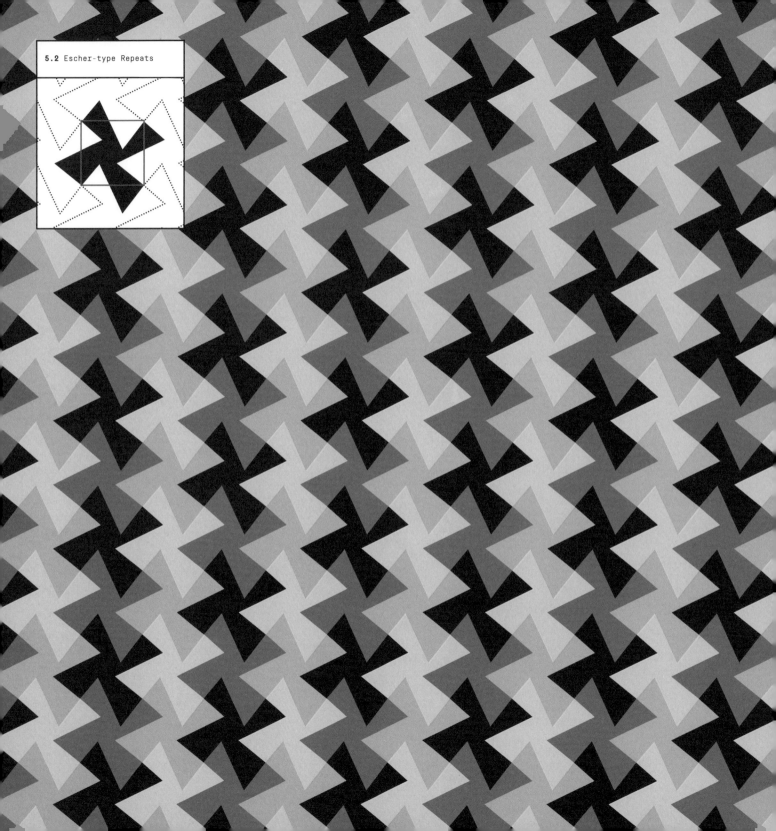

5.2 Escher-type Repeats

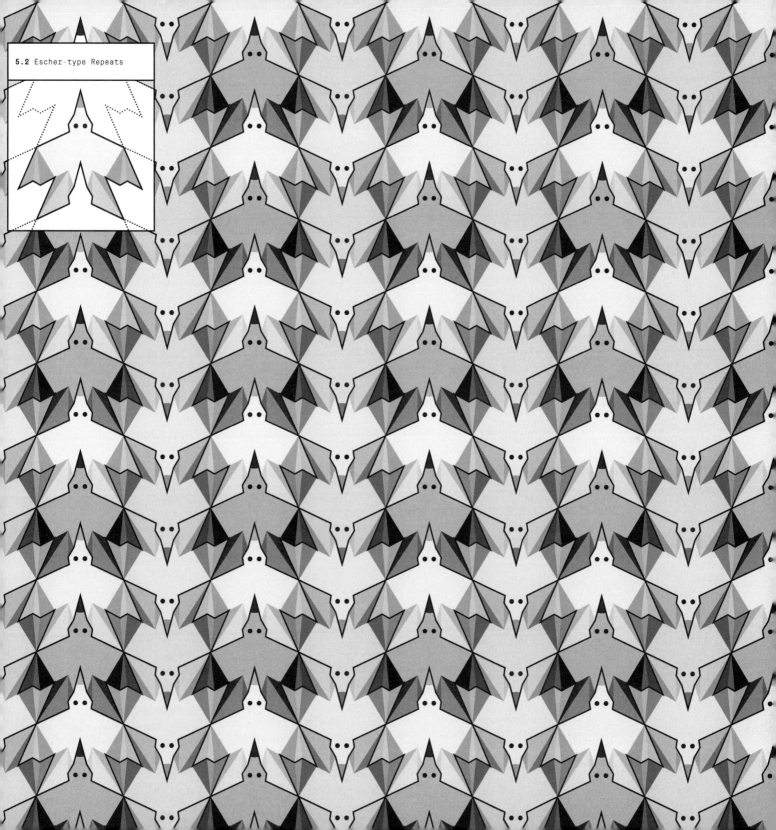

5.2 Escher-type Repeats

5.2 Escher-type Repeats

Triangular Tiles and Planar Tiling
In this second method of tiling triangles, all three sides of the triangle are deformed so that the tiles can cover a plane in a simple grid.

(1) In the examples on pages 138–143, tiles were created by deforming opposite sides of a square or rectangle, so that as one side became convex, the opposite side became correspondingly concave. However, triangles do not have opposite sides, so this method will not work. The trick is to first define the corners and then also the midpoints of each side with a series of dots.

(2) Deform a side outwards on one half of one side of the triangle and correspondingly inwards on the other half. Each half is a 180-degree rotation of the other half.

(3) Repeat the deformation on the other two sides, observing the same rules. There are many ways to deform the side of the triangle but, as always, be careful not to create angles that are too narrow or corners that are too tight.

(4) This is the final outline of the tile without the lines that define its triangular structure.

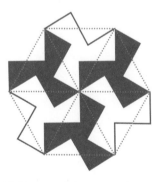

(5) Six tiles are placed together rotating around a central point (an order 6 rotation – see page 24).

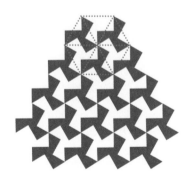

(6) This is the final grid of triangular tiles.

(7) There are many possible variations, including curved edges and tiles that curl around others at the corners. However, not all the sides need to be identical. The final example shows three different sides. Note how each side still follows the half-convex, half-concave rule that ensures it will exactly abut its neighbours on all three sides. Note also how this final variation is not rotational like the other repeats in this example, but an illustration of translation symmetry. Turned one way, the tile looks like a rabbit, and from another like a sailboat with a rudder. With a little work, it should be possible to make the tiles more representational. It is also possible to have just two different sides, meaning that two sides will be identical and the third side will be different.

5.2 Escher-type Repeats

Hexagonal Tiles

Hexagonal tiles are a hybrid. They use the geometry of equilateral triangles, but because they have an even number of sides (six), they can be subjected to the opposite and alternating symmetry operations of squares and rectangles. Also, because three angles of 120 degrees meet at a corner, three colours must be used to render the repeat pattern, not two.

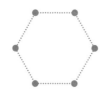

(1) Here are six dots that define the corners of a hexagon.

(2) Deform one of the sides into the body of the hexagon. There are many ways to do this, but for clarity the example shown here is simple.

(3) Repeat the same deformation on alternate edges of the hexagon.

(4) Fill in the incomplete tile so it can be seen more clearly.

(5) Place it inside a bounding hexagon.

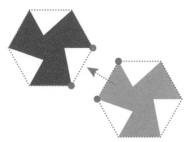

(6) Create a copy of the previous step, but change the colour of the fill. Bring the two hexagons together, so that a coloured edge on one hexagon lies against a white edge of the other.

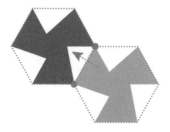

(7) A white shape will be trapped between the two hexagons. In this example, the shape is triangular. Expand the coloured edge of one of the tiles across the hexagonal boundary so that it occupies the white shape.

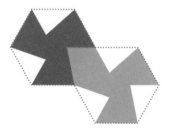

(8) This is the result. Notice how the light blue tile now buts against the dark blue tile.

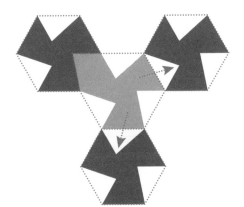

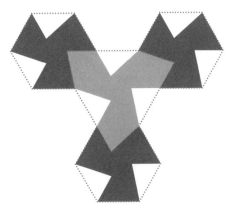

(9) Repeat the last three steps twice more, expanding the light blue tile into the white spaces next to two other dark blue tiles.

(10) This is the result. The light blue tile is now complete.

(11) Stripped of the boundary lines, this is how the light blue tile will look. The same steps are now performed on the dark blue tiles.

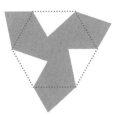

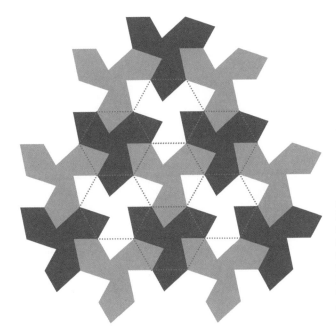

(12) An analysis of the light blue tile will reveal that the three shapes outside the hexagonal cell are the same as the three white voids inside the cell. It is this 'give and take' that enables the pattern of connected hexagonal tiles to repeat successfully. Each tile, however oddly shaped, has exactly the same area as one whole hexagon.

(13) Here is the repeat pattern. Note how the light and dark blue tiles create white tiles that are the same shape as themselves. Thus, three colours are needed to render the pattern. The original grid of hexagons is difficult to see, but when it is overlaid, the structure of the repeat is clear.

Learn the Rules ... Break the Rules

It is often said that rules have to be learned before they can be broken. To create spontaneously without following rules might show a commendable degree of imaginative thinking, but it could also be described as indulgent doodling. Unfettered spontaneity can mean a lot to its creator, but it does not always communicate much to anyone else.

On the other hand, to create following only a given set of formulae and conventions – the 'rules' – also communicates little. Slavish rule-following can be as empty as rule-less creativity.

All successful designers – in fact, creators of all kinds, from painters to composers and from to poets to architects – create a language that is unique and identifiable to them. A language is a set of rules, but they are rules devised by the creators themselves and they constantly evolve with each new piece. There is an interesting philosophical discussion to be had here about whether creativity resides primarily in freedoms or restrictions. But what is its connection with this book?

Simply this: the book should be read with care. It is vital to learn the ways in which repeat patterns are made using the four basic symmetry operations described in Chapter 1, and then using the more complex operations described in the following chapters. It is then important to apply what has been learned to a series of designs using a variety of media, so that the symmetry operations can be tested and evaluated.

However, once these rules have been learned, it is vital to break them and try to create repeat patterns in ways not suggested in the book. When rules are broken in the full knowledge of which rules are being broken and why, the resulting work can be informed, intelligent and witty, rather than indulgent and incommunicative.

So, you have read the book and understand how to make repeat patterns in the correct way. What rules could you try to break? On the opposite page you will find a few ideas, though you could also come up with a few of your own.

Omit Some of the Elements in a Repeat

Not every element – or even every motif or meta-motif – in a repeat needs to be used. Some of them can be omitted, perhaps randomly or perhaps in an organized repeat.

Add a Rogue Element

When making a repeat pattern, instead of repeating the same element, motif or meta-motif, add a second one. It can be placed randomly, or in a repeat pattern.

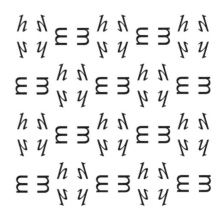

Combine Two Symmetry Operations – or More

The pairing of two different symmetry operations will add much interest to a repeat. The two operations can be similar – such as two operations that use 90-degree geometry – or very different, such as 90- and 120-degree operations.

Use a Different Motif for Every Repeat

A motif can itself be a repeat pattern, so to place different motifs in a grid retains the essence of a repeat, without actually creating a repeat pattern within the grid. The effect can be an interesting mix of the chaotic and the ordered.

Make Every Element Different

Instead of making just one element and repeating it, make a collection of different elements and use them just once each. This will not make a repeat pattern, but will at least make a grid. By repeating some of the elements, the semblance of a pattern can be made.

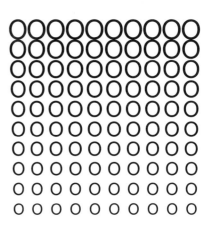

Change the Scale

Instead of keeping a repeat at the same scale across the surface, try gradating it larger or smaller from one edge to another. Alternatively, keep the scale consistent, but gradate the distance between the repeats.

Symmetry Operation Reference Finder

For easy reference, here are the seven linear and seventeen planar symmetry operations. Seeing them grouped together should help you see the similarities and differences between them and help you choose which operation to use.

Linear Symmetry

2.1 Translation [p.40]

2.2 Translation + Vertical Reflection [p.42]

2.3 Translation + 180-degree Rotation [p.44]

2.4 Translation + Glide Reflection [p.48]

2.5 Horizontal Reflection [p.50]

2.6 Vertical Reflection + Translation
+ Horizontal Reflection + 180-degree Rotation [p.52]

2.7 Translation + Vertical Reflection
+ 180-degree Rotation + Vertical Reflection [p.54]

Planar Symmetry

3.1 Translation [p.58]

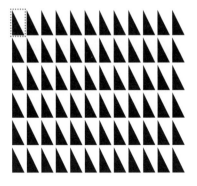

3.4 Reflection
+ Parallel Glide Reflection [p.66]

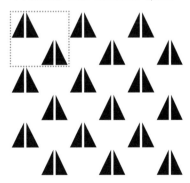

3.2 Glide Reflection [p.60]

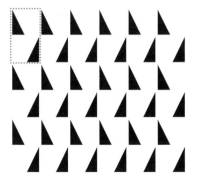

3.5 180-degree Rotation [p.70]

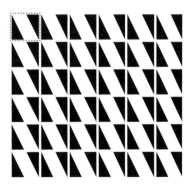

3.3 Double Reflection [p.64]

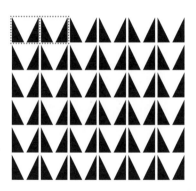

3.6 Reflection
+ Perpendicular Glide Reflection [p.72]

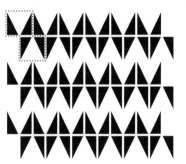

Symmetry Operation Reference Finder

3.7 Two Perpendicular Glide Reflections [p.76]

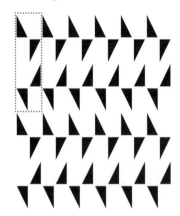

3.8 90-degree Reflections around a Point [p.78]

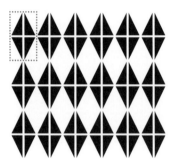

3.9 Reflection + Rotation + Reflection
+ Perpendicular Reflection [p.82]

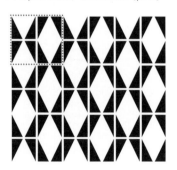

3.10 Three 120-degree Rotations [p.84]

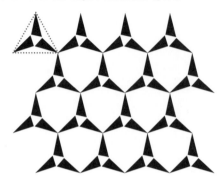

3.11 Reflections in an Equilateral Triangle [p.88]

3.12 Reflections of 120-degree Rotations [p.90]

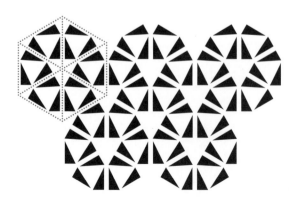

3.13 90-degree Rotations [p.94]

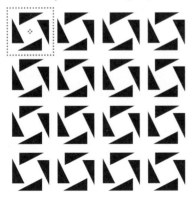

3.14 Reflections of 90-degree Rotations [p.96]

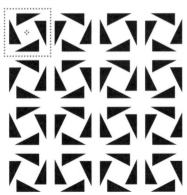

3.15 Reflections of a 45-45-90-degree Triangle [p.100]

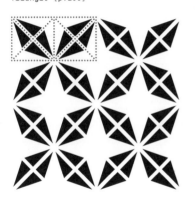

3.16 60-degree Rotations [p.102]

3.17 Reflections on the Sides of a 30-60-90-degree Triangle [p.106]

Glossary

This is a glossary of the technical words and phrases used in the book. The definitions give meanings that relate specifically to symmetry and pattern making and may differ from general definitions. If a word is capitalized, it or a closely related word is defined elsewhere in the glossary.

Asymmetrical
A Figure which is not Symmetrical.

Axis
An imaginary Point or line about which a Figure Rotates or Reflects.

Cell
A Polygon that enables a Repeat Pattern to repeat across a Surface. The shape of the Polygon is predetermined by the shape of the Element, Motif or Meta-motif that it contains. (See also Tiling.)

Deforming
A process by which the sides of a simple Figure such as a Polygon are made more complex, but the corners remain in fixed positions:

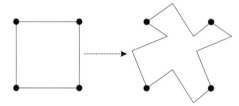

Element
The smallest part of a Repeat Pattern. Elements combine to create a Motif.

Equilateral Triangle
A triangle in which all sides are the same length and all angles are 60 degrees.

Escher-type Repeats
Named after the Dutch graphic artist M.C. Escher (1898–1972), these are intricately designed Tiles that depict living creatures, human figures and objects.

Euclidean Geometry
A collection of self-evidently true geometric propositions (such as that parallel lines never meet) developed by the Greek mathematician Euclid, ca. 300 BCE. They form the basis of modern geometry.

Figure
A Two-dimensional graphic image.

Fractal
A Figure in which the characteristics of its details are repeated at larger scales.

Frequency
The number of times something repeats over a given distance. (See also Spacing.)

Glide
Another word for Translation Symmetry. (See also Slide.)

Glide Reflection Symmetry
The combination of two Symmetry Operations. First, a Translation Symmetry operation is made, followed by a Reflection Symmetry operation in the same direction as the Translation.

Grid
A Repeat Pattern created when two or more rows of identical lines intersect each other at different angles:

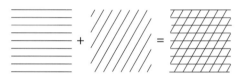

Half-drop Repeat
A Repeat Pattern created when alternate rows of a repeated Element, Motif or Meta-motif are placed halfway between the Figures in the rows above and below:

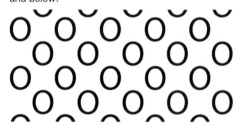

Isosceles Triangle
A triangle in which two sides and two angles are equal.

Linear Symmetry
Symmetry Operations repeated in a line.

Line of Reflection
An imaginary line across which a Figure reflects.

Meta-motif
The combination of two or more Motifs.

Mirror Image
When one half of a Figure is the Reflection of the other half. (See also Reflection Symmetry.)

Motif
A Figure composed of two or more Elements.

One-dimensional
A singularity. A zero-dimensional point without height, width or depth. (See also Point.)

Operation
An action. (See also Symmetry Operations.)

Order 2 / Order 3 / ...
The dividing of 360 degrees into equal parts. Order 2 means to divide 360 degrees into two parts, thus each part is 180 degrees. In order 3, each part is 120 degrees – and so on. It is used in Rotational Symmetry.

Orientation
The relative position of one Figure in relation to another, often referred to by degrees of relative separation.

Perpendicular
A line or Figure at 90 degrees to another.

Plane
A flat, Two-dimensional Surface with height and width, but no thickness.

Planar Symmetry
Symmetry across a Two-dimensional Plane.

Point
A zero-dimensional singularity without height, width or depth. (See also One-dimensional.)

Point Symmetry
See Rotational Symmetry.

Polygon
A closed Two-dimensional shape made of straight lines, such as a square.

Quadrilaterals
Any Polygon with four straight lines.

Repeat Pattern
A repeat pattern is created when a Figure is repeated according to one of the Symmetry Operations.

Reflection Symmetry
When one half of a Figure is the Mirror Image of the other half. (See also Mirror Image.)

Rhombic
A Quadrilateral in which opposite sides are parallel and no corner is 90 degrees.

Rotation
The act of rotating around a central Point or Axis. (See also Axis.)

Rotational Symmetry
The duplication by Rotation of a Figure around a central Point.

Scalene Triangle
A triangle in which the three sides and the three angles are different.

Scaling
To enlarge or diminish a Figure.

Seamless Repeat
A Repeat Pattern apparently without a clear beginning or end, or any obvious boundary between the repeats. Otherwise known as a Wallpaper Repeat.

Semi-regular Tiling
Tiling patterns created when Tiles that do not fit perfectly together across a Surface create secondary Polygons in the spaces between the Tiles:

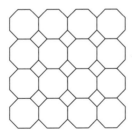

Slide
Another word for Translation Symmetry. (See also Glide.)

Spacing
The distance between repeats. (See also Frequency.)

Stepping
Repeatedly moving to the side in a series of equal upwards or downwards steps:

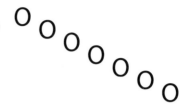

Surface
A flat Two-dimensional Plane.

Symmetry
When a Figure copies itself and the duplicate Slides, Rotatations or Reflections are relative to the original.

Symmetry Operations
The four ways to create Symmetry: Rotational, Translation, Reflection and Glide Reflection Symmetry.

Tessellation
Cells or Tiles that fit together across a Plane, without gaps.

Three-dimensional
An object that exists in space, that has height, width and depth.

Tiles
Identical Polygons that repeat across a Two-dimensional Plane and fit together without gaps.

Translation Symmetry
The movement of a Figure (that is, an Element, Motif or Meta-motif) a described distance in a described direction. The distance and angle between the Figures remain constant and the Figures neither Rotate nor Reflect.

Two-dimensional
A flat Plane with height and width, but no thickness.

Wallpaper Repeat
A Repeat Pattern apparently without a clear beginning or end, or any obvious boundary between the repeats. Otherwise known as a Seamless Repeat.

Acknowledgements

Those readers who recognize my name will probably know me as the author of books about paper folding for designers. Only recently did I realize that my knowledge of how to manipulate paper was based on a strong but mostly intuitive understanding of how to use the laws of symmetry to create repeat patterns of folds. For this reason, I must thank the many origami artists, pop-up artists and students who over the years, have unintentionally taught me an affinity with symmetry and pattern.

Professor Peter Stebbing convinced me that a book about symmetry and pattern written for designers could and should be written and that it was me who must write it. Without his enthusiasm and faith, this book would not have been conceived.

The repeat patterns used in the book were originated under my guidance by students from Degree-level Design courses at the Hochschüle für Gestaltüng in Schwäbisch Gmünd, Germany, then developed and recoloured by the book's designer, Nicolas Pauly. I thank the students for their dedication and beautiful work. They are: Sofie Ascherl, Julia Böhringer, Dennis Ehret, Franziska Fink, Lisa Kern, Manuel Goetz, Felix Gräter, Josh Greaves, Paul Kaeppler, Sascha Kurz, Lee Cheng-Yu, Carla Lenné, Annabel Müller, Yannik Peschke, Tabea Scheib, Jakob Schlenker, Mara Schmid, Lina Stadelmaier, Janis Walser-Cofalka, Leonie Weiss and Philine Winkler. My thanks to Vice-Rektor Professor Ulrich Schendzielorz at the HfG, for permission to work with the students.

I must also thank my editor, Sara Goldsmith, for her exceptionally keen eye and great editorial abilities, the book's designer, Nicolas Pauly, for his clear layouts and easy-to-understand repeat patterns and my wife Miri Golan, for her patience when, yet again, I left the laundry undone under the pretext of working on the book.